London
The Cookbook

Frances Lincoln Limited
74–77 White Lion Street
London N1 9PF

London *The Cookbook*
Copyright © 2017 Quintet Publishing Limited

First Frances Lincoln edition 2017

A catalogue record for this book is available from
the British Library.

ISBN 978-0-7112-3827-5

Quintet Publishing Limited
Ovest House
58 West Street
Brighton BN1 2RA
United Kingdom

Designer: Lucy Smith
Art Director: Michael Charles
Editorial Director: Emma Bastow
Publisher: Mark Searle

Printed in China

1 2 3 4 5 6 7 8 9

London
The Cookbook

The story of London's world-beating food scene, with
50 recipes from restaurants, artisan producers and neighbourhoods

CARA FROST-SHARRATT
FOREWORD BY FERGUS HENDERSON

F
FRANCES
LINCOLN

Contents

Foreword

One begins to wonder how big London's appetite can get, as the tummy of the great metropolis grumbles more and more. Eateries grand, plain and simple, or strangely complicated, with every country represented. All are trying to stem this massive hunger. I myself seem to have contributed to this quagmire of kitchens in a mother hen kind of way (cluck cluck), shooing my chickadees out of the nest when they are ready to flee the coop.

With all these new restaurants opening I find the creature of habit in me comes to the fore. I must have bored many people over the years about my love of lunch at Sweetings – working chaos in action; a joy to behold. This glorious institution is something that could never be designed; if you did it would seem trite and boring (not to mention senseless), but somehow here the tolerance of surfaces of the old wet fish shop that the restaurant inhabits allows for the rigours of a good lunch.

Also an old favourite is Ikeda on Brook Street. This was a Japanese restaurant before Japanese restaurants became as ubiquitous and homogenised as they so often are today. Here is sushi on blood-temperature rice, dishes of herbs and roots, and an open kitchen which cooks at a purposeful pace, which is hypnotic to watch.

Since you are getting my Pop Picker's Favourites, here is Le Gavroche – for me the home of comfort. The waiters glide, you glide yourself, and indeed everything glides once you are in. There was one occasion on which the gliding got the better of me: lunching with a friend after a late night, Chef de Rang was slicing our chicken and I dropped off just as he was about to sauce my plate. I woke with a start just before I hit the chicken with my nose and before I received an earful of sauce. Disaster was averted, though it left both me and the waiter a bit shaky.

Excuse me if I seem a little insular when it comes to the London food scene. I assure you that this is not the case. You are as likely to find me in the delightful BAO as at Cipriani. On the other hand, I am a chap who was described in one of St. John's first reviews as being 200 years out of date.

I have a cabbage theory, based on an evening that I spent in Rome with some young groovers who spent the whole night discussing punterelle, the Roman bitter green chicory. The day I hear London hipsters talk about an English cabbage with such love I will know that London has truly become as food-aware as it feels. I think we are getting there – those small farmers' markets sprouting up all over the city give one hope. For example, Kennington, the market nearest us at home, sells extra thick raw cream, which is wonderful when scooped liberally onto pudding. Then there is the butcher who, when asked whether he had any more lamb's kidneys, replied that the lamb only has two. These are life-affirming moments.

Fergus Henderson

Introduction

London is renowned the world over for the quality, diversity and ingenuity of its food. It has taken time and no small effort from an army of dedicated restaurateurs, food purveyors and producers to achieve this coveted reputation but the city is now a top culinary destination with a food scene that matches its magnetic pull of history and culture.

From street food stalls to Michelin restaurants, London is a magnet for cooking talent: a place where, no matter the cuisine or the credentials of the restaurant, there is always an appetite for good food. Chefs are keen to experiment with new concepts, while diners are open to trying diverse national and regional cuisines from all over the globe. London is a city where pretty much anything is possible when it comes to food: palates are challenged, skills are pushed to the limit and ambitions are realised.

London has a resurging craft beer industry, with pubs and bars keen to stock locally produced ales, lagers and ciders; while the capital is also becoming home to an increasing number of food producers who appreciate the camaraderie, community, local appetite and environmental benefits of basing their businesses on their customers' doorsteps.

Food markets are vibrant and thriving, with artisan and farmers' markets in practically every corner of the capital – from stalls setting up in school car parks, to the mighty Borough. And night markets are becoming the new hipster hangout; street food, music and cocktails providing the backdrop to a weekend in the city.

Brewers, bakers, smokers, conservers, distillers, beekeepers, coffee brewers and cheesemakers all have their part to play in keeping Londoners' appetites whetted with exciting new, local ingredients. Meanwhile, restaurateurs and chefs come up with ever more interesting ways to prepare and present the array of ingredients that are sourced not only from the capital but also from every corner of the globe.

This book showcases the best that London has to offer, from some of the brightest stars in the restaurant industry to some of the most exciting food purveyors living and working in the capital. There's a comprehensive overview of the best food markets, as well as introductions to some of London's neighbourhoods where the rich history of the city has resulted in diverse ethnic culinary hubs. There are restaurants featured all over the city – from classic establishments to new eateries that have been quick to make an impression. Then it's time to meet some food producers – people who have chosen to set up their businesses in the capital and connect with a network of likeminded individuals.

There are recipes from chefs, market traders, pop-up restaurants and food producers, which highlight the creative talents of the individuals, as well as the diversity of the food scene. These will give you a taste of what London has to offer so you can experience the food and soak up the atmosphere of the restaurants, markets, cafes and bars that make this city so special.

Cara Frost-Sharratt

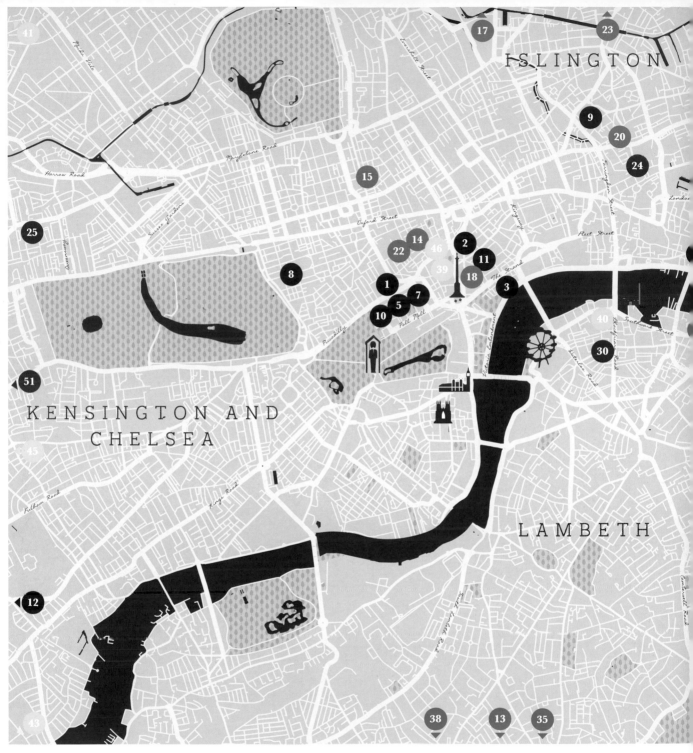

T O W E R
H A M L E T S

G R E E N W I C H

LONDON CLASSICS

As capital cities go, London is one of the greats – if not the greatest. It's got it all: an illustrious history, iconic and centuries-spanning architecture, a diverse cultural offering and, without doubt, the most eclectic and exciting collection of restaurants you're likely to stumble across anywhere in the world.

A number of London restaurants have been satiating the hunger of their patrons for generations – some for hundreds of years. They have defied the odds by surviving wars, revolts and political turbulence but, perhaps most importantly, the often fickle and constantly evolving food scene. And yet, they have continued trading, many with menus that only deviate slightly from when they first opened and interiors that have been tastefully updated but remain true to their historical roots and their place in London's culinary timeline.

But it's not simply days ticked off the calendar that sets these stalwarts apart; so much more is involved. It's the consistency of the food and service, the painstaking attention to detail, the dedication to excellence and the dose of unadulterated and life-affirming joy that accompanies each meal. That's why this collection of greats has a loyal following – patrons who dine here regularly; settling down to a meal with the relaxed familiarity of stepping into a favourite pair of slippers, coupled with the absolute certainty that the meal will be sublime.

Bentley's has been shucking oysters since 1916 and remains one of the best seafood restaurants of the capital; The Ivy is the dinner joint of choice for the capital's glitterati; and Le Gavroche has been turning out Michelin plates of food for half a century under the proprietorship of the Roux family. And there's no reason to believe that any of them will be hanging up their aprons any time soon.

Bentley's Oyster Bar & Grill

11–15 Swallow Street W1B 4DG
+44 (0)20 7734 4756 / www.bentleys.org

What is arguably London's best-known fish restaurant is hidden between the tourist thoroughfares of Regent Street and Piccadilly, where it has been quietly, elegantly and successfully serving its loyal clientele since it first opened its doors in 1916.

When you step inside, you could be forgiven for thinking you'd travelled back in time – although the restaurant and bar has undergone many incarnations and makeovers, the opulent interior still pays homage to the halcyon days of early twentieth-century drinking and dining. Bentley's has always drawn a sophisticated crowd – from theatregoers and shoppers popping in for drinks and snacks in the ground-floor bar, to those entertaining guests or conducting business meetings in the more formal upstairs dining room.

As the name of the restaurant suggests, it's the oysters that draw in the diners above all else on the menu. The kitchens were originally stocked with oysters from the Bentley family's Colchester oyster beds and the restaurant can lay claim to taking what had been considered a staple for London's poorer classes and transforming it into a sought-after culinary superstar.

By sticking to a short and simple menu, Bentley's has succeeded in maintaining its well-earned reputation for no-fuss food of exceptionally high quality. While it has witnessed the rise and fall of many neighbouring establishments, Bentley's has stayed the distance by pleasing returning customers with its consistency and quality. The Oyster Bar menu is all about the oysters – which are sourced from across the British Isles and Ireland – as well as caviar and ceviche. The grill menu centres on fish, with enough meat dishes to satisfy carnivores, while an ever-changing market menu showcases the best seasonal ingredients.

Bentley's has seen a number of owners over its lifetime, the most recent being Bentley's custodian, Michelin-starred chef Richard Corrigan, who bought Bentley's in 2005 with a view to upholding its fine reputation. His ethos of sourcing the best-quality ingredients and offering a fresh, simple menu has ensured the continued success of this London stalwart. A sympathetic updating of the interior has kept the original design features prominent, with the era celebrated rather than dumbed down by a modern overhaul. With such careful conservation of its history and culinary values, it's easy to imagine diners still enjoying the delights of Bentley's in another 100 years.

Opening times	Tube	Bus
Mon–Sat 11:30am–11:30pm **Sun** 11:30am–10:30pm	Piccadilly Circus	14, 19, 22, 38, N19, N22

Bentley's
Oyster croque monsieur

SERVES 2

4 slices white bread
200 g (1¾ sticks) butter
8 oysters (shucked, juices reserved)

For the mustard and Tabasco sauce:
100 g (½ cup) butter
100 g (¾ cup) flour
500 ml (2 cups) milk
1 tbsp English mustard
12 drops green Tabasco
salt and pepper, to season

The croque monsieur is said to have originated in Paris in the early 1900s after a brave café proprietor replaced the customary baguette with sliced white bread for the lunch menu. It's essentially a ham and cheese sandwich but with a very Gallic twist that involves frying the humble bread in generous quantities of butter. Here, Bentley's has taken the snack to another dimension with oysters bathed in a mustard and Tabasco sauce.

Prepare the sauce. Melt the butter in a medium pan, add the flour and cook for about 5 minutes, whisking vigorously, until a paste forms.

Pour in the milk and continue whisking until the sauce simmers and no taste of flour remains

Add the mustard, Tabasco and oyster juice. Season lightly with salt and pepper and set aside to cool.

Butter the bread with half of the butter. Spread a thin layer of cooled sauce on two slices of bread. Place 4 oysters on each of these slices, on top of the sauce, and place the other slices of bread on top (butter-side down), forming a sandwich.

Cut into quarters and pan fry in the remaining butter until the sandwiches turn golden on both sides.

The Ivy

1–5 West Street WC2H 9NQ
+44 (0)20 7836 4751 / www.the-ivy.co.uk

The go-to haunt of film executives, publishers and anyone who wants everyone to know where they've been for dinner, The Ivy is the darling of Covent Garden. The restaurant has built a hugely successful reputation based on its perfectly executed combination of glitz and quality – patrons feel spoilt by the surroundings, the service and the food.

Its location in the heart of London's theatreland certainly helps The Ivy to massage the egos and satiate the appetites of the rich and famous – bag yourself a reservation and you never know who might be sitting on the next table – but a restaurant is only as good as the food it serves. Having been around since 1917, it's safe to say that quality is an ongoing theme with a menu based on classic and contemporary ingredients and dishes.

Original owner Abele Gandolini wanted to create a cosy enclave for discerning diners who didn't want over-stylised dishes with lengthy descriptions and ingredients lists that required a dictionary. From the beginning it was all about quality classic dishes; comfort food with a Hollywood makeover. So, while you might choose an Asian sharing platter, you're just as likely to be tucking into Shepherd's Pie, Crackling Roast Pork or Grilled Dover Sole, and rounding off your meal with a Knickerbocker Glory.

Although the paparazzi might be hanging around outside, the interior is a welcome respite from glaring eyes and flashing cameras. The famous stained glass windows offer privacy to those who require it, and the warm, wood tones, panelling and luxurious furnishings create a welcoming and homely environment – a cocoon of coolness in the centre of town. Regular guests are treated like old friends and it's a testament to the service and food that so many return time and again.

Although part of the large Caprice Holdings group, The Ivy – and indeed all the group's restaurants – has a unique identity and appeal. This famous restaurant has been filled with famous people for nearly one hundred years and it shows no sign of slowing down.

Mon–Wed 8am–11:30pm		
Thur–Fri 8am–12am		
Sat 12pm–12am		
Sun 12pm–10:30pm		
	Leicester Square	49, 211, 11, 19, 22, N11, N19
Opening times	**Tube**	**Bus**

The Ivy
Shepherd's pie

SERVES 6

200 g (7 oz) lean rib of beef, minced
    (ground)
200 g (7 oz) lean lamb, minced (ground)
2 shallots, peeled and finely chopped
100 g (3½ oz) button mushrooms, brushed
    off and finely chopped
1 medium carrot, finely chopped
3 sprigs fresh thyme, leaves removed
1 tbsp tomato paste
200 g (7 oz) canned chopped tomatoes
100 ml (½ cup) red wine
1 tbsp plain flour (all-purpose)
2 tbsp Worcestershire sauce
300 ml (1¼ cups) veal stock (if not available,
    use beef or chicken stock)
3 sprigs fresh oregano, leaves removed
    and chopped
sunflower oil, for frying
salt and freshly ground black pepper,
    to season

For the topping:
1 kg (2 lb) King Edward, Maris
    Piper or russet potatoes
50 g (¼ cup) unsalted butter
salt and white pepper, to season

One of the most striking things about The Ivy is its all-encompassing menu, providing succour for all tastes. Influences are drawn from childhood, international cuisine and great British staples and the Shepherd's Pie is famous. Indeed, thousands of Ivy Shepherd's Pies have passed the lips of thespians and others down the decades. Nursery food par excellence, The Ivy's version uses minced lamb and beef, making it a hybrid of shepherd's and cottage pies. The ingredients render it rich and deeply satisfying.

Lightly oil both the lamb and beef. Heat a frying pan until smoking and cook the mince, stirring constantly, for about 5 minutes, until the meat is a light brown colour. Pour off the excess liquid and transfer to a dish until the rest of the ingredients are ready.

In the same pan, heat a little oil and gently sweat the shallots, mushrooms, carrots and thyme for about 8 minutes. Add the mince and tomato paste and cook for about 5 minutes. Add the chopped tomatoes and red wine and reduce for about 10 minutes. Add the flour and mix thoroughly. Add the Worcestershire sauce and stock, bring to the boil and simmer for 30 minutes.

Season, add more Worcestershire sauce if required, and then add the oregano. Stir, remove from the heat and keep to one side. Preheat the oven to 180°C (350°F).

For the topping, peel and cut the potatoes into even-sized pieces. Cook in boiling salted water for around 15 minutes until soft. Drain and return to the pan over a gentle heat to remove any excess moisture. Using a potato masher or ricer, thoroughly mash the potatoes, mix with butter and season to taste.

Spoon the meat mixture into an ovenproof dish, or divide equally between 6 individual dishes. Top with the mashed potato (you can pipe this if you like) and bake in the oven for about 30 minutes. It should turn a nice golden colour.

At The Ivy, we serve the pie with buttered peas and carrots.

Simpson's-in-the-Strand

100 Strand WC2R 0EW
+44 (0)20 7836 9112 / www.simpsonsinthestrand.co.uk

The Grand Divan – the dining room at Simpson's – is as impressive as it sounds and takes its name from its original incarnation as a coffee house and chess club called Reiss' Grand Cigar Divan that opened on the site in 1828. During this time, the practice of carving joints of meat at the table was introduced so serious chess players could dine during lengthier games without disruption and, although the chess players moved elsewhere, the tradition continues to this day.

Another legacy of stocking the kitchens with British produce also remains and Simpson's is a true, original supporter of native produce and suppliers, including the signature 28-day aged Roast Rib of Scottish Beef. Other popular items on the menu include Roast Saddle of Lamb, Native Oysters, Traditional Steak and Kidney Pie (and Pudding) and Pot Roasted Partridge. The seasonal menus are packed full of British standards that are, for the large part, unashamedly rich, hearty and classic.

It's a menu that hasn't radically altered since the restaurant first came to the attention of London's nineteenth-century fine diners and continued to curb appetites over the decades (and centuries) that followed. If an establishment can appeal to diners across such a great span of time by serving the same style of food in the same surroundings, it's clearly got a winning formula and Simpson's rightly decided to keep this intact. Obviously, there have been nods to modernity since the likes of William Gladstone – and Charles Dickens before him – took their seats in the dining room and perused the menu. However, the surroundings, impeccable service and championing of the British classics have remained unchanged.

Simpson's offers a glimpse into London's rich culinary past, both in terms of the food and the opulent décor once you step inside. Coffered ceilings, large chandeliers and luxurious patterned carpets create a memorable atmosphere that is made even more memorable once the food arrives. And, if you long to be able to carve your Sunday roast as expertly as the chef that brings your meat to the table, you can book one of the carving courses that are held at Simpson's on Sundays throughout the year.

Mon–Fri 7:15am–10:30am, 12pm–2:45pm, 5:45pm–10:30pm		
Sat 12pm–2:45pm, 5pm–10:30pm		
Sun 12pm–9pm	Temple	6, 9, 1, 4, 26, N1, N9
Opening times	**Tube**	**Bus**

Simpson's-in-the-Strand
Roast rib of beef

SERVES 8–12

For the beef:

1 tbsp sea salt

1 tbsp freshly ground black pepper

2 tbsp English mustard powder

4–5 kg (9–11 lb) beef forerib

For the Yorkshire puddings:

275 g (2¼ cups) flour

450 ml (2 cups) full-fat milk

5 medium eggs

vegetable oil, for baking

salt and pepper, to season

For the horseradish cream:

200 g (7 oz) English horseradish

50 g (2 oz) wild Swedish horseradish

1 tsp white wine vinegar

200 ml (¾ cup) mayonnaise

25 ml (1½ tbsp) double (heavy) cream

salt and pepper, to season

Nothing shouts British classics like roast rib of beef and Simpson's is a stalwart when it comes to culinary heritage. The kitchen uses 28-day dry-aged forerib for this oft-requested dish and advises home cooks to visit the local butcher rather than the supermarket when buying the beef. Request an oven-ready forerib but with the feather bones tied back so they act as a trivet while the meat is roasting.

Preheat the oven to 165°C (330°F) (this temperature ensures a moist rib of beef).

Mix together the salt, pepper and mustard powder. Rub this mix all over the joint (fat and meat) but avoid the bones (if you use them for gravy the mix can make it bitter).

Place the joint in a large, deep roasting tray, rib bones down, so they act as a trivet. The rib bones should be the only part of the joint in direct contact with the tray.

Place the tray in the oven. After 1 hour, check the core temperature of the beef – you're aiming for 35°C (95°F). It will need longer than 1 hour but checking now helps to work out roughly when the correct temperature is reached.

When the beef reaches temperature, remove it from the oven, wrap lightly in kitchen foil and allow to rest for the same time that it was cooking. The bones act like a radiator and keep the meat warm, while the core temperature will rise and retain the juices.

Yorkshire puddings (makes 12)

Combine the flour, milk and 3 of the eggs in a large bowl and season with salt and pepper. Leave to rest overnight (or at least 3 hours) in the fridge.

Add the remaining 2 eggs to the batter and whisk well to combine.

Preheat the oven to 190°C (375°F).

Pour a layer of vegetable oil into a 12-hole muffin tray. Pour the batter into the tray and cook for 20 minutes.

When the yorkies are ready, open the oven door and leave them to stand in the oven for a further 10 minutes.

Horseradish cream

Peel and grate the English and Swedish horseradish into a small bowl. Season with salt and pepper, add the vinegar and mix well to combine. Cover and place in the fridge for 1–2 hours.

Remove from the fridge, add the mayonnaise and cream and mix well to combine.

Sweetings

39 Queen Victoria Street EC4N 4SF
+44 (0)20 7248 3062 / www.sweetingsrestaurant.co.uk

Sweetings has been serving seafood to City gents since 1830 (and since 1889 from its current premises near Cannon Street). It's a place that revels in being old fashioned without being pompous, a right earned by having survived two World Wars and more financial crashes than you can shake a crab claw at.

The restaurant takes pride in upholding its traditions: it refuses to take bookings (although it has become inadvertently fashionable by doing so), keeps its (strictly French) wine list brutally short and pours beer in pewter tankards. Although it now has a website and a Twitter account, it only dropped its cash-only policy and introduced a credit card machine shortly before the dawn of the 21st century.

The dining room is a mixture of mosaic-tiled floor, wooden panelling, marble counters, linen-draped benches and blue leather upholstered stools. Its walls are hung with old photographs, caricatures and framed knick-knacks. The room invariably fills up swiftly when the doors open at 11.30am, its clientele a sea of suits that like to celebrate their successes and soothe failures with Burgundy, Bordeaux and Champagne. Get there any later than midday and you're unlikely to get a seat.

Sweetings doesn't have a menu, it has a stubbornly retro bill of fare, currently overseen by head chef Alex Beck, which includes West Mersea oysters, crab bisque, smoked eel, potted shrimps, fried whitebait, prawn cocktail and lobster thermidor. Main courses run from extravagant fresh catches such as turbot and Dover sole, to the infinitely more affordable fish pie. Puddings are hefty British classics such as steamed syrup pudding, baked jam roll and spotted dick. If you're not sweet of tooth or still hungry they still give space to the notion of 'Savouries' to finish, with rarebits and roes on toast to soak up the last of your wine.

Sweetings doesn't serve dinner, it doesn't open at weekends and it doesn't serve coffee – it never has done and (hopefully) never will.

Mon–Fri 11:30pm–3pm **Sat–Sun** Closed	Mansion House	11, 15, 17, N15, N199
Opening times	**Tube**	**Bus**

Sweetings
Fillet of hake with a lobster mash

SERVES 2

300 g (10 oz) Maris Piper or russet potoates
    peeled and cut in half

2 tsp salt

50 ml (¼ cup) double (heavy) cream

2 tbsp butter, plus extra for frying

150 ml (⅔ cup) lobster bisque
    (see recipe below), plus extra to serve
    (optional)

100 g (4 oz) diced cooked lobster tail

15 g (½ cup) chopped fresh parsley, plus
    extra to garnish

2 x 200 g (7 oz) hake portions (skin on)

vegetable oil, for frying

salt and freshly ground black pepper, to
    season

lemon wedges, to serve

tartar sauce, to serve

For the lobster bisque:

275 g (9 oz) lobster claws and body shells

100 ml (½ cup) olive oil

2 tbsp unsalted butter

50 g (⅓ cup) chopped onion

2 garlic cloves, chopped

50 g (⅓ cup) chopped carrot

50 g (¼ cup) chopped leek

50 g (½ cup) chopped celery

5 parsley stalks

3 tbsp tomato paste

125 g (4½ oz) canned chopped tomatoes

2 ltr (8 cups) fish stock

50 ml (3 tbsp) brandy

50 ml (¼ cup) double (heavy) cream

2 tbsp cornflour (cornstarch), diluted with a
    little water

Fish and seafood are frequent visitors on Sweetings' bill of fare and head chef Alex Beck treats his ingredients with the utmost respect. Here, fillets of hake are simply fried in butter and oil and served alongside creamy mash combined with a punchy lobster bisque.

Place the potatoes in a pan, cover with water, add the salt and bring to a boil. Simmer for 15–20 minutes. Drain in a colander, then place over the hot pan to remove excess water. Leave for 5 minutes. Pass through a potato ricer, or mash.

Bring the cream and butter to the boil in a pan. Add to the mash and mix well.

Heat the lobster bisque and add the cooked lobster tail. Heat through then add to the mash. Season, add the parsley and mix well.

Heat a little oil in a non-stick frying pan, season the fish on both sides and place in the pan, skin-side down. Hold the fish in place for 30 seconds to colour the skin. Cook for about 6–7 minutes, until golden brown. During cooking add a knob of butter and baste.

Turn the fish over and cook for about 2 minutes. When cooked the middle should be almost white. For well done, cook for 1 minute more.

To serve, place a quenelle of mash on the plate and lean the fish against it. Serve with lemon wedges and sprinkled with fresh parsley. Accompany with tartar sauce and a little lobster bisque, if liked.

Lobster bisque

Preheat oven to 200°C (400°F). Crush the lobster claws and shells thoroughly.

Add the olive oil to a large roasting tray and place in the oven. When the oil is close to smoking point, add the claws and shells. Tip them away from you, stir and return to the oven. They need to be as brown as possible but not burnt – about 30 minutes. Stir occasionally.

In a large pan, add the butter, vegetables and parsley and sweat for about 5 minutes. Add the tomato paste and chopped tomatoes, mix well and simmer on a low heat for 5 minutes. Add the fish stock and bring to the boil. Reduce to a simmer and cook for 20 minutes, stirring.

When the claws and shells are browned, add to the pan and add water to cover, if necessary. Bring back to the boil then reduce to a gentle simmer. Reduce by about one-third.

In a small pan, warm the brandy. Tilt the pan away from you, move back, carefully ignite the brandy and flambé. When the flame has disappeared, add the cream and bring back to the boil. Whisk in a little cornflour to thicken. Simmer for 5 minutes then add to the bisque and stir. Pass the bisque through a potato mouli.

The Wolseley

160 Piccadilly W1J 9EB
+44 (0)20 7499 6996 / www.thewolseley.com

The Wolseley hasn't always been a restaurant: originally designed as a car showroom for The Wolseley Car Company, the building then went on to become a bank until it was finally transformed into the plush eatery that caters to every palate at every meal, from breakfast to late-night snacking.

Its central Mayfair location and diverse food offering attracts a diverse range of diners who gather for business breakfasts, shopping lunches, celebratory afternoon teas and romantic dinners. And it's this huge range of dining options that keeps the restaurant lively, fresh and top of the radar for people watching. The vast open dining room manages to be opulent yet understated at the same time: first-time visitors will be taken aback by the high ceilings, elaborate staircase and the sheer scale of the room, which is filled with the buzz of diners' conversations.

The all-day dining ethos means there's never really a quiet time at The Wolseley, with breakfast, lunch and afternoon tea menus seamlessly taking over from each other throughout the day against the backdrop of the constant day menu. Here, you'll find soups, salads and hot sandwiches, as well as a number of bistro-style stalwarts such as grilled fish, burgers and spinach tart. However, it's breakfast that really steals the show: whatever you fancy, you can pretty much guarantee that it's on the menu; whether that's a pot of tea and a pastry, kedgeree, devilled kidneys or a full English – it's all there.

Despite its prestigious postcode, kerb appeal and delightful interior, The Wolseley is accessible and welcoming – there are no airs and graces and the prices are reasonable considering the quality, attention to detail and impeccable service that comes with every cover. It's versatile eating with a large side order of class that has proven to be a winning formula for locals and visitors alike.

Mon–Fri 7am–12am		
Sat 8am–12am		
Sun 8am–11pm	Green Park	14, 19, 22, 38, N19, N22
Opening times	**Tube**	**Bus**

The Wolseley
Eggs Benedict

SERVES 2

4 free-range, organic eggs
4 English muffins
4 slices Yorkshire ham
butter, for muffins
good pinch cayenne pepper
good pinch chopped chives
salt, to season

For the hollandaise sauce:
(makes about 250 ml/1 cup):

4 tbsp white wine vinegar
2 shallots, coarsely chopped
10 peppercorns
175 g (1½ sticks) butter, cut into cubes
3 egg yolks
juice of ½ lemon
salt, to season

CHEF'S TIP:

If the sauce should separate at any point, beat a fresh egg yolk with a spoonful of water in a clean bowl. Whisk the separated sauce into the egg and it should magically come back to a smooth sauce.

Eggs Benedict is a very popular dish at The Wolseley – we sell over 2,000 a month. Its inception is hotly debated but most agree that the dish was created in New York at the end of the 19th century during the American renaissance.

One story I like is that of Lemuel Benedict, a retired Wall Street stockbroker. He wandered into the Waldorf Hotel in 1894 and, hoping to find a cure for his morning hangover, ordered 'buttered toast, poached eggs, crisp bacon and a hooker of hollandaise.' The maître d'hôtel, Oscar Tschirky, was so impressed with the dish that he put it on the breakfast and lunch menus but substituted ham and a toasted English muffin for the bacon and toast.

The key to a great hollandaise is great ingredients. Look for very fresh eggs that are local, free range and organic with a deep yellow yolk. The quality of the ham is also imperative – choose Yorkshire ham. Lastly, avoid supermarket muffins, as they tend to be doughy. Either make them yourself or go to your local bakery.

Maarten Geschwindt, Head Chef

First make the sauce: put the vinegar, shallots and peppercorns in a pan and bring to the boil. Continue to boil until the sauce is reduced to about two-thirds. Strain into a glass bowl.

Clarify the butter by melting it in another heavy pan over a gentle heat. Skim the surface until only clear liquid remains. Remove from the heat and allow to settle and cool until tepid. Carefully pour out the clarified butter into a bowl, leaving any solid residue behind.

Place a round, heatproof bowl over a pan of simmering water. Add the egg yolks and the reduction. Beat the mixture over the heat until it forms a smooth, thick, pale mass. Remove from the heat and whisk vigorously (in the same direction), adding enough of the clarified butter to make a thick, creamy sauce. Adjust the flavour with a little lemon juice and salt, to taste. Keep warm.

Poach the eggs in a large pan of water for 3–4 minutes and remove with a slotted spoon. Toast the muffins under a medium grill, first removing a thin slice from the top of each. Keep the grill on.

Butter the muffins and arrange the ham on top. Press a spoon into the muffins to give the egg a neat hollow to sit in. Briefly return under the grill to warm.

When the eggs are cooked, drain well and season with salt. Place them in the muffin hollows and spoon over the sauce. Sprinkle with cayenne pepper and chives.

M. Manze

87 Tower Bridge Road SE1 4TW / 105 High Street SE15 5RS / 226 High
Street SM1 1NT +44 (0)20 7277 6181 / www.manze.co.uk

M. Manze is a real family affair, having been established by Michele Manze in 1902 and
now owned by his grandchildren. Michele's family emigrated from Italy and swapped ice
cream for pie and mash when they set up the first shop in Bermondsey.

It was a savvy move, as Londoners at the time craved affordable and filling food and the
simple menu of jellied eels and pie, mash and liquor perfectly suited the wallets and taste
buds of the local working-class population. The popularity of Manze's handmade pies
led to the opening of several more shops and, although some of these failed to survive the
bombing during WW2, the Bermondsey and Peckham branches remain.

As tastes changed and fast food chains claimed more of people's lunch money,
traditional pie and mash shops went into decline and it was the older generation that
largely kept the tills ticking over. However, M. Manze not only survived the fast-food
revolution, but the family also proved that there was still an appetite for this fare and
opened another shop in Sutton, south London, in 1998. This coincided with a culinary
U-turn that saw Londoners once again take pride in their food heritage and embrace
traditional dishes with a sense of nostalgia and a new appreciation.

In terms of value for money, you'd be hard pressed to beat the heaped plates of food that
are assembled swiftly and identically from the trays of handmade pies, and great pans of
mash that is freshly prepared on site every day. This is no-frills eating – hearty food with a
soul. Simple tables and bench seating make best use of the space and, with such a succinct
menu, turnaround is quick – even when the Saturday lunchtime queue stretches out the
door. You're not given any reason to linger; this workaday pie shop does what it says on the
tin and, no sooner has the final spoon of mash soaked up the last drop of liquor, customers
are on their feet and on their way.

Mon 11am–2pm		
Tue–Thur 10:30am–2pm		
Fri 10am–2:30pm	⊖	🚌
Sat 10am–2:45pm	Borough	42, 1, 188, N1
Opening times	**Tube**	**Bus**

M. Manze
Traditional pie-shop pies

MAKES 2

For the pastry:
225 g (1¾ cups) plain (all-purpose) flour
pinch of salt
75 g (⅓ cup) lard
75 g (⅓ cup) butter

For the filling:
1 beef stock cube
350 g (12 oz) lean minced (ground) beef
¼ tsp salt
¼ tsp pepper
milk, to glaze

For the mash:
2 large potatoes (such as Maris Piper or
    russet), chopped
125 ml (½ cup) full-fat milk
2 tbsp butter
salt and pepper, to season

For the parsley liquor:
2 tbsp butter
2 tbsp cornflour or plain flour
300 ml (1¼ cups) chicken stock
handful freshly chopped parsley

The exact recipe for the pies sold in M. Manze shops is a closely guarded secret and it would be very difficult to replicate in a domestic kitchen – they produce hundreds of pies every day. This tailor-made version is simplicity itself to prepare at home and is the ultimate comfort food.

In a large bowl, mix the flour with the salt and rub in half of the lard. Add enough cold water to bring the flour to a soft dough. In a separate bowl, mix together the rest of the lard and the butter.

Roll out the dough to make a rectangle 12.5 x 25 cm (5 x 10 inches).

Dot one-third of the butter and lard mixture over two-thirds of the rectangle. Fold the third without any fat on it over the middle third of the pastry. Bring the other third on top. Seal the edges with a rolling pin and turn the dough 90 degrees. Chill for 10 minutes.

Repeat with half of the rest of the fat and then repeat one more time with the remaining fat. Chill for 10 minutes after each folding.

Roll and fold one more time without any fat and then chill for 30 minutes.

For the filling, crumble the stock cube and dry-mix all of the ingredients in a large bowl and put to one side.

Roll out the pastry to a thickness of about 1–2 mm (⅛ inch) and cut into 4 pieces. Take 2 small greased pie dishes and lay 1 piece of pastry over each. Push the middle of the pastry down to make room for the filling.

Put half the filling in each dish and pour enough water in to cover the meat – this will make your gravy.

Wet the edge of the pastry base to allow the top to stick to it and then place the second piece of pastry on top and press down lightly. Trim the pastry back to the edge of the dish and glaze with a small amount of milk. Place the pies to one side to rest for 30 minutes.

Preheat the oven to 190°C (375°F). Place the pies in the oven and cook for about 30–35 minutes until golden brown.

Prepare the mash: boil the potatoes in a large pan of water. Drain thoroughly and mash with the milk and butter. Season with salt and pepper, cover and set aside.

Prepare the liquor: melt the butter in a medium pan. Gradually whisk in the cornflour until it forms a thick paste. Drizzle in the stock, whisk well and simmer gently for a couple of minutes. Stir in the parsley.

To serve, spoon some liquor onto serving plates. Carefully remove the pies from the dishes and place on the plates, along with a generous scoop of mashed potato.

Fortnum & Mason

181 Piccadilly W1A 1ER
+44 (0)20 7734 8040 / www.fortnumandmason.com

This iconic store on Piccadilly started life in 1707 as a comparatively modest grocer's shop. Founded on the profits from recycling royal candles by the thrifty William Fortnum – a footman in the household of Queen Anne – who convinced his landlord, Hugh Mason, to open a small shop with him on St James Market. His palace connections helped ensure that the business prospered and it grew to become London's leading food emporium. Its position as a royal supplier was cemented by Fortnum's grandson, Charles, who went into service for Queen Charlotte. Today, it is the holder of warrants from the Queen and the Prince of Wales.

From fuelling campaigning soldiers in the Napoleonic wars, to introducing Heinz Baked Beans to an enthusiastic British public, Fortnum & Mason has a history as rich as the beef tea they dispatched to Florence Nightingale's hospital in Crimea on Queen Victoria's orders in the aftermath of the Charge of the Light Brigade.

However, although famed for its loose-leaf teas – as well as confectionery and luxury hampers (which were graciously sent to the suffragettes imprisoned for breaking Fortnum's windows in 1911) – it will forever be linked with one famous British staple and that is the Scotch egg. This breaded, sausage-meat-encased boiled egg has, in recent years, gone from languishing in convenience store chiller cabinets, to being reinvented by gastro pubs as the ultimate bar snack, served hot from the fryer.

While it may actually have its origins in a Mughal dish, Fortnum's claims to have invented the Scotch egg in 1738. Originally designed as handy portable sustenance for travellers heading west out of London by coach, it – unlike the 'meat lozenge', another Fortnum's invention – has stood the test of time. You'll find many variations on sale in Fortnum's today, with eggs encased in black pudding or salmon, or featuring jalapeño peppers. However, the following recipe is based on the traditional version made with pork sausage meat.

Mon–Sat 10am–9pm	⊖ ⊖	14, 19, 22, 38, N19, N22
Sun 12pm–6pm	Piccadilly Circus	
Opening times	**Tube**	**Bus**

Scotch eggs

MAKES 4

150 g (5 oz) Scottish white pudding

150 g (5 oz) premium pork
  sausage meat

2 sprigs rosemary, finely chopped

½ tsp sea salt

pinch of white pepper

5 medium organic eggs (at room
  temperature)

50 g (½ cup) plain (all-purpose) flour

150 g (1 cup) panko Japanese breadcrumbs

3 tbsp semi-skimmed milk

vegetable oil, for frying

Created by Calum Franklin (head chef at Holborn Dining Room), this recipe won the 'Traditional' category at the 2015 Scotch Egg Awards. This take on the classic recipe uses white pudding for extra richness and panko breadcrumbs, which result in a light but crispy texture.

Crumble the white pudding into the sausage meat with the rosemary, sea salt and white pepper. Mix well and then divide into balls weighing 70 g (3 oz) and place in the fridge to chill.

Bring a large pan of water to the boil, place 4 of the eggs in the pan and boil for 5½ minutes. Remove and put in a bowl of water with plenty of ice. Leave for 5 minutes to cool completely and then peel and dry.

Take 3 bowls: put the flour in one, the breadcrumbs (lightly crush some in your hands for texture) in another and the remaining egg, beaten with the milk, in the final bowl. Remove the sausage balls from the fridge, flatten and wrap evenly around the eggs, making sure the egg is snug in the meat.

Dip in the flour and dust off any excess. Dip in the egg mix and finally in the breadcrumbs, coating all over. Preheat the oven to 180°C (350°F).

In a deep pan or wok, heat enough vegetable oil to cover the eggs and fry for 1½ minutes, until golden brown. Remove and place on an oven tray and bake in the oven for 5 minutes.

Allow to rest for 1 minute before eating.

Le Gavroche

43 Upper Brook Street, W1K 7QR
+44 (0)20 7408 0881 / www.le-gavroche.co.uk

Somewhat ironically, Le Gavroche – Victor Hugo's street urchin character in his novel *Les Miserables* – far surpasses its humble namesake. Over half a century old, it first opened its doors in Lower Sloane Street when it began life as a family restaurant belonging to the now-famous Roux brothers, Albert and Michel. During the sixties and seventies it received widespread critical acclaim at a time when French cuisine on the London culinary scene was alarmingly underwhelming by today's high standards.

Thus firmly established, Le Gavroche quickly expanded and in 1981 moved to its current location. Soon after, it won its third Michelin star, making it the first restaurant in the country to have achieved the much-coveted hat-trick. Thanks to its renowned authenticity and impeccable attention to detail, it has comfortably retained its position in the upper echelons of modern haute cuisine. In 1991 Michel Roux Jr. took over and remained loyal to his father's founding principles of French culinary expertise while adding his own signature to its distinctive menu, ensuring the restaurant's constant acquisition of prestigious awards and accolades over the decades and right up to the present day.

The formula behind Le Gavroche's unrivalled success is actually very simple: the provision of the very best of French cuisine combined with bold and unique twists to ensure the menu is exciting while remaining true to the philosophy that underpinned its origins. As a result, a dining experience here is not cheap. However, thanks to the introduction of set lunch menus, it is now more accessible and is enjoyed by more visitors than ever before. For those looking for an exclusive experience, the restaurant also offers private dining for up to six people, with a daily changing six-course menu and live video link directly into the kitchen for those keen to watch their dishes being created.

Le Gavroche's global reputation is maintained thanks to the high standard of its impressive menu as well as its exquisite service – the result of years of research, hard work and perfectionism, of the sort most high-end restaurants can only dream of achieving. Food critics relish the chance to review cuisine that's arguably off the scale when it comes to ratings. Le Gavroche ticks all the boxes.

Opening times	Tube	Bus
Mon–Fri 12pm–2pm, 6pm–10pm **Sat** 6pm–10pm **Sun** Closed	Marble Arch	30, 72, 84, 94, 137

Moro

34–36 Exmouth Market EC1R 4QE
+44 (0)20 7833 8336 / www.moro.co.uk

Exmouth Market is firmly on the London food map and its pedestrianised street lined with bars and restaurants makes it ideal for idle wandering and lingering over a long meal. On more clement days, you could be forgiven for thinking you were on a city break in a continental hotspot and a table at Moro will add fuel to your foreign fantasy – especially if the table is outside.

With its Moorish menu of Spanish and North African food, this stylish restaurant filled a void that London hadn't quite realised was there. Moro was founded by husband and wife team Sam and Sam Clark – who learned first-hand about these unique south Mediterranean ingredients and cooking techniques by travelling and tasting their way around the region.

Meat is wood-roasted or chargrilled to create a rich, smoky flavour in exotic dishes that are described so delightfully that it's difficult to pinpoint a favourite: ingredients like pomegranate molasses, wild garlic leaves, rose harissa and roasted sour plums are sprinkled across the menu like choice pickings at a Mediterranean food market. An all-day tapas menu is served in the bar for those who want to sample as many flavours and ingredients as possible. And there's also the option of popping next door to Moro's little sister Morito, which has even more choice of tapas and mezze. As one would expect, there's a fine selection of Spanish and Portuguese wine and cava to choose from, as well as sherries, some of which can be paired with the desserts and cheeses that finish the menu.

The restaurant is warm and inviting with hints of accent colour rather than an overpowering explosion. Bar stools and dining furniture serve their purpose rather than demand attention and this all adds up to a kind of rustic minimalism that ensures the focus is always on the food and the atmosphere created by the diners enjoying it.

Mon–Sat 12pm–2:30pm, 6pm–10:30pm **Sun** 12:30pm–2:45pm	Angel	63, N63, 19, 341
Opening times	**Tube**	**Bus**

The Ritz

150 Piccadilly W1J 9BR
+44 (0)20 7493 8181 / www.theritzlondon.com/ritz-restaurant

When The Ritz first opened its doors in 1906 it quickly gained a reputation as one of London's most prestigious hotels. It remains an iconic name today, oozing glamour and sophistication and attracting tourists and locals in equal measure. First-time visitors can be seen gazing open-mouthed at the unashamedly decadent interior that includes frescoes, opulent furnishings, chandeliers, palms and elegant facades at every turn.

The Ritz Restaurant is a culmination of the hotel's style and it prides itself on being among the most lavish hotel dining rooms in the world. It therefore seems fitting that the restaurant was established by Auguste Escoffier, arguably one of the greatest chefs in history. The food befits its grand surroundings and the menu takes the best British ingredients and transforms them into sumptuous dishes. There are many tributes to the classics – Loin of Lamb, Roast Partridge and Crepes Suzette, to name a few – but there is always an extra flourish or the addition of exotic or extravagant ingredients to remind diners of the pedigree of their surroundings and the chefs. The team in the kitchen is led by Executive Chef John Williams, who oversees all the hotel's restaurants and ensures consistency, which is all-important for returning guests.

Dining at The Ritz is so much more than simply sitting down and ordering a meal. The experience begins when you enter the hotel doors – the setting, the service and the incredible food make it a far more memorable occasion than dining elsewhere. Traditional dinner dances are still held in the restaurant at the weekends so that guests can enjoy the lavish surroundings of the dining room for even longer, as they swap food for fancy footwork once the dessert plates have been cleared away.

Mon–Sat 7am–11am, 12:30pm–2:00pm, 5:30pm–10pm
Sun 8am–11:00am, 12:30pm–2:00pm, 7pm–10pm

Green Park

9, 14, 19, 22, C2

Opening times

Tube

Bus

47

Rules

35 Maiden Lane WC2E 7LB
+44 (0)20 7836 5314 / www.rules.co.uk

Rules is justifiably proud of the accolade of being London's oldest restaurant. However, perhaps more impressive is the consistent popularity it has enjoyed since opening in 1798. Patrons are staunchly loyal to the old-school service and a menu that has been tweaked and updated but has essentially changed little over the last 200 years.

It's a menu that celebrates all things British, with a particular emphasis on game, hearty pies and shellfish. Rules is something of a champion of British game and, as the range and quality of these native ingredients has become more appreciated among diners and chefs, so Rules has enjoyed an even greater patronage.

Book a table for dinner and you can choose from dishes such as Saddle of Rabbit, Spatchcocked Squab Pigeon or Roast Loin of Venison. Classic fish dishes like Fillet of Lemon Sole also grace the menu but this certainly isn't the place to book if you're dining with vegetarians. Although the lack of any vegetarian option (bar a couple of salads) might be considered archaic in today's culinary climate, this refusal to detour from tradition is part of Rules' charm. Diners choose the restaurant for its hearty take on classic British ingredients and there is clearly no need to clutter up the kitchen with anything that hasn't been shot or caught: should patrons forget, there's even a warning on the menu that game birds may contain lead shot.

During its 200-year history, Rules has been in the ownership of just three families, which helps to explain the unswerving dedication to tradition. The décor reiterates this, with crisp white table linen against a backdrop of brocaded banquettes and dark wood furniture. The walls are tightly packed with an eclectic collection of art that reflects the long and illustrious history of the restaurant.

While culinary tastes have evolved over the decades, and restaurants constantly change hands and change menus, Rules has barely wavered from its original concept and is proudly traditional – flying the flag for British ingredients prepared to perfection.

Mon–Sat 12pm–11:45pm		
Sun 12pm–10:45pm	Covent Garden	6, 9, 11, 14, N9, N11
Opening times	**Tube**	**Bus**

River Café

Thames Wharf, Rainville Road W6 9HA
+44 (0)20 7386 4200 / www.rivercafe.co.uk

In recent years, the incredible culinary achievements of the River Café have been somewhat outshone by the fact that chef-owner Ruth Rogers 'discovered' Jamie Oliver. Although true to an extent (Oliver did indeed find his chef feet in the kitchens of the restaurant, where he worked for over three years), it's also fair to say that all well-known chefs had to work their way up the ranks and River Café is a destination restaurant that has given a boost to the careers of many rising stars.

Luckily, the original reasons that the River Café was so feted have returned to the fore, and the Hammersmith-based restaurant that resides on the bank of the Thames has never been so popular. Opened in 1987 by Ruth and the late Rose Gray, the restaurant originally operated as a staff canteen for the next-door architect practice of Ruth's husband Richard Rogers. Despite its non-central location and the lack of formal training on the part of the founders, the quality of the food was sufficient to propel the restaurant to greatness – in 1998 River Café received a Michelin star.

The ethos behind River Café was to bring a breath of fresh air to the London Italian food scene, with authentic recipes using exceptional ingredients that were carefully sourced. This remains true today and, as well as being seasonal, the menus change daily. Fresh pasta is paired with herbs, seasonal vegetables, cheeses and shellfish, while main courses see fish take a starring role, alongside prime meat cuts and artisanal ingredients. The restaurant's cheese room offers an incredible selection of the best regional Italian cheeses, while the range of gelati includes flavours such as Pear & Grappa, Roasted Almond, and Chocolate.

The dining room is light, bright and spacious, with an open kitchen that blurs the boundaries between chefs and diners. But if you have an insight into the unpredictable British weather and manage to bag a table on a clement day, the gorgeous garden terrace is the only place to enjoy lunch or dinner – Tuscany on the Thames.

Mon–Thur 12:30pm–2:15pm, 7pm–9pm
Fri 12:30pm–2:15pm, 7pm–9.15pm
Sat 12:30pm–2.30pm, 7pm–9.15pm
Sun 12:00pm–3pm

Barons Court

190, 211, 220, N11, N97

Opening times

Tube

Bus

NEW CLASSICS

Hundreds of restaurants open every year in the capital but it takes more than a large bank balance and an empty space in a prime location to create a truly successful eatery.

Restaurateurs and chefs need to carve out a niche that sets them apart from the competition while also steering clear of the fads and food fetishes that see many establishments open to a blaze of glory and fade to obscurity a few months later.

This last decade has seen many exciting developments in London's food scene, with the surging popularity of farmers' markets, easy access to previously hard-to-source ethnic ingredients and a burgeoning pride and interest in traditional and new-wave British food. Meanwhile, the proliferation of pop-up restaurants and supper clubs has enabled budding restaurateurs to test the waters and diners to become acquainted with lesser-known cuisines.

As Londoners develop an ever more sophisticated palate and are spoilt for choice when it comes to eating out, with meals that are tailored to wallets of every girth, so it becomes increasingly difficult for talented chefs to achieve acclaim. This makes the restaurants in this chapter particularly special.

They have harnessed the magic formula of passion, creative genius, hard work and a deep understanding of, and respect for, the changing nature of trends and tastes. On top of that, they have survived the wrath of the critics' pens –pleasing columnists and pulling in bread-and-butter punters is no mean feat.

More than ever before, food is so much more than simply fodder – whether dining out or eating in, greater consideration is taken over what and where to eat and these restaurants are part of this new culinary landscape and they have every intention of staying put.

The Dairy

15 The Pavement, Clapham Old Town SW4 0HY

+44 (0)20 7622 4165 / www.the-dairy.co.uk

Clapham has been quietly and confidently elevating itself to become a true contender on the London food scene – the independent shops on Northcote Road are of the highest order, while a smattering of Michelin stars in and around the area prove there's dedication to excellence in SW4.

One of the new stars on the block is The Dairy, which was opened by chef Robin Gill and his wife in 2013. Although his cooking heritage is top notch (The Oak, Le Manoir aux Quat'Saisons), Robin was by no means an industry name when he went all out to open his own restaurant. But it seems that his focus on squeezing out every last morsel of flavour from every morsel of his carefully sourced ingredients paid off and The Dairy soon became a destination restaurant, not only for Clapham but also for all corners of the capital.

The menu – which is developed by Robin and head chef Richard Falk – is divided into clear-cut sections that include Garden, Sea, and Land, as well as a dedicated Vegetarian section that will make non-carnivores weep with joy at having a selection of dishes to choose from (what's not to like about Nika Beetroot Tartare served with smoked yolk and nasturtium capers?). Dishes are small plates so you can select from each section and order according to your appetite. Alternatively, the tasting menu offers incredible value for money for the amount of food that's delivered to the table.

The appearance of cuttlefish, smoked eel and veal on the menu demonstrate Robin and Richard's affinity with quality ingredients that have often been overlooked or shied away from. And there are extra personal touches like the herbs and salad leaves that are grown on the roof (yes, there's an edible roof garden in the heart of Clapham) to the little extra courses that randomly appear during the meal.

With the sister restaurant, The Manor, also taking Clapham by storm, and cute little snack bar Counter Culture right next door, Robin seems to be making all the right moves to cover all bases in this South London food destination.

Opening times	Tube	Bus
Mon Closed **Tue** 6pm–10pm **Wed–Fri** 12pm–3pm, 6pm–10pm **Sat** 10am–3pm, 6pm–10pm **Sun** 10am–3pm	Clapham Common	50, 155, 35, 37, 345

The Dairy
60-day aged beef tartare with sour onions and nasturtium capers

SERVES 2

For the sour onions:
300 g (10 oz) roscoff onions, peeled and
  quartered
½ tsp salt
300 ml (1¼ cups) whey

For the nasturtium capers:
1 tbsp salt
300 ml (1¼ cups) water (for the brine)
100 g (4 oz) nasturtium buds
100 ml (½ cup) water (for pickle liquid)
100 ml (½ cup) white wine vinegar
1 tbsp caster (superfine) sugar

For the oyster emulsion:
100 g (4 oz) shallots, peeled and sliced
200 ml (¾ cup) dry white wine
125 g (4½ oz) fresh chucked rock oysters,
  juice reserved
150 ml (⅓ cup) grape seed oil
oyster juice, to loosen sauce

For the shallot crisps:
150 g (1½ sticks) butter, diced
150 g (5 oz) banana shallots, peeled and
  finely sliced
salt, to season

For the beef tartare:
250 g (9 oz) 60-day aged beef rump,
  trimmed and diced
1 tbsp Dijon mustard
1 tbsp nasturtium caper juice
1 tbsp extra virgin olive oil
handful nasturtium leaves
salt and freshly ground black pepper,
  to season

The success of this recipe comes down to the quality of the beef. After that, it's all about presentation – the delicate nature of the ingredients calls for a creative touch.

Sour onions (prepare 1 month in advance)
Place the onions into a jar with a seal-tight lid. Mix the salt with the whey and pour over the onions. Seal the jar and place in a storecupboard, out of daylight, to ferment for 1 month. They are ready when the onion starts to break down and they are acidic.

Nasturtium capers (prepare 1 week in advance)
Add the salt to the brine water in a pan. Bring to the boil until the salt is dissolved then cool. Take a third of the brine and soak the buds for 24 hours. Drain, wash with cold water and repeat this process over 3 days. On the third day prepare the pickle liquid by adding the remaining ingredients to a pan. Bring to the boil, dissolve the sugar, then pour the liquid over the buds. Leave for at least 3 days.

Oyster emulsion (prepare on the day)
Add the shallots to a pan, pour over the wine and place on a low-medium heat. Boil until the wine has evaporated, remove and chill. Add the shallot mix and oysters to a blender and blend until smooth. Gradually add the oil until the mix is mayonnaise consistency. Add a little oyster juice to loosen the mix. Keep refrigerated until plating.

Shallot crisps (prepare on the day)
Place the butter in a wide, flat-bottomed pan on a high heat. Stir until the butter starts to foam. Add the shallots and cook, stirring, until the shallots start to brown and the butter smells like roasted nuts. Remove the pan from the heat and strain the shallots through a sieve. Spread the shallot crisps on a flat tray on kitchen paper and season lightly with salt. Keep in a warm, dry place.

Plating the beef
Add the beef to a mixing bowl with the mustard. Season with salt, pepper and the nasturtium caper juice and finish with olive oil. Place a large spoon of the oyster emulsion in the centre of the plates and spread it over the base of the plates with the back of a spoon. Scatter over the tartare, followed by a generous spoon of the nasturtium capers. Next add the sour onion, in slices, over the top. Dress some nasturtium leaves in the beef mixing bowl, add to the plates and finish with shallot crisps.

Koya Bar

50 Frith Street W1D 4SQ
www.koyabar.co.uk

London loves Japanese food – from fine dining restaurants like the estimable Ikeda to no-frills noodle bars like Koya. And, when it comes to the latter, Koya Bar is the best. This popular Soho eatery stands apart with its authenticity and focus on freshly cooked fare that has flavour crammed into every bowl and plate. There are tables, bench seats and little else in the way of décor or adornments in the pared-back, café-style interior but you won't notice – all your focus will be on the food.

As a noodle bar, the star of the show in Koya is the udon noodle and you can enjoy these thick wheat noodles hot or cold in a broth, or served with a sauce, and with a variety of ingredients and toppings – from vegetable tempura or smoked mackerel to mushrooms or fermented soy beans. There's also a selection of small plates on the menu, to whet your appetite while the noodles are being prepared – or to keep them company – and here you'll find tempura, salads, pickles and miso soup.

If you've never tried Japanese food for breakfast, Koya Bar is the place to begin your adventure – and okayu (porridge) is the item to order. Forget oats and milk; this version is made from rice and is served with pickles and a soft-boiled egg.

Koya Bar sits comfortably in its Soho surroundings and serves its purpose wonderfully, with a steady flow of customers that swells at lunchtime and forms an orderly queue out of the door. As you'd expect, there are no reservations, so it's a case of first come first served, and you'll either be seated at the bar or filtered onto one of the communal tables. If you do show up during a busy lunchtime you won't mind waiting, as you'll be hard-pressed to find fresher, tastier and better value Japanese food anywhere in town.

Opening times	Tube	Bus
Mon–Wed 8:30am–10:30pm **Thur–Fri** 8:30am–11pm **Sat** 9:30am–11pm **Sun** 9:30am–10pm	Leicester Square	14, 19. 38, N19, N38

Koya Bar
English breakfast

SERVES 2

4 rashers smoked streaky bacon

4 shiitake mushrooms

3 tbsp butter

2 tbsp olive oil

2 eggs

soy sauce, to season

For the fish dashi (makes 900 ml):

1 tbsp kombu

900 ml (4 cups) water

2 tbsp katsuobushi (bonito flakes)

For the miso soup:

reserved kombu and katsuobushi

350 ml (1¼ cups) water

2 tbsp miso paste

100g (4 oz) tofu, cut into small cubes

1 spring onion (scallion), finely sliced

For the rice porridge:

125 g (½ cup) rice

840 ml (3½ cups) water

salt, to season

This is a popular choice on the Koya Bar menu. The main dish is served in a bowl and is accompanied by miso soup and rice porridge. You will need to make a batch of fish dashi for the miso – the quantity is sufficient for six servings.

Fry 2 rashers of bacon and 2 mushrooms in a non-stick frying pan (without oil), until cooked through and golden, turning once. Set aside on a plate.

Place half the butter and 1 tablespoon of the olive oil in the pan and scrape off any bacon bits with a wooden spatula.

Turn the heat to minimum and gently place an egg in the pan. Add the bacon and shiitake around the egg and cover the pan.

Fry until the edge of the yolk is just cooked and carefully transfer the food to a plate. Repeat with the remaining ingredients for the second serving.

Season with soy sauce and serve with miso soup and rice porridge.

Fish dashi

Wipe the kombu with a clean, damp cloth. Transfer to a large pan, add the water and soak for 30 minutes.

Place the pan over a low heat and, as the kombu starts to lift up to the surface, add the katsuobushi. Turn off the heat and leave for 5 minutes. Drain through a sieve (reserve the kombu and katsuobushi to make miso soup).

Miso soup

Place the leftover kombu and katsuobushi (from the fish dashi) in a small pan with the water and cook over a medium heat. Set aside for 5–10 minutes and then drain through a sieve.

Add the miso paste, tofu and spring onion and stir.

Rice porridge

Wash the rice in cold water a few times until the water runs clear.

Place the rice in a large pan with the water and put on maximum heat on the hob. When it comes to the boil, turn down the heat to minimum. Stir the rice from the bottom of the pot a couple of times and cover with a lid with a slight opening.

Cook for a further 40 minutes and season with a pinch of salt at the end of the cooking time.

Portland

113 Great Portland Street W1W 6QQ
+44 (0)20 7436 3261 / www.portlandrestaurant.co.uk

Portland opened its doors and its kitchen in early 2015, and has quickly put its name on the London restaurant map as a destination venue for exceptional food that manages to be both creative and fuss free.

The central Marylebone location and diminutive size of the restaurant mean it's constantly buzzing and you're unlikely to be able to wander in for a table on spec. But booking means you can anticipate the meal and that's no bad thing in the case of Portland.

The brainchild of Will Lander (Quality Chop House) and Daniel Morgenthau (10 Greek Street), the menu takes the best of British and international food offerings and elevates them to something extremely special. The daily menu is broad enough to make choosing difficult but small enough to ensure total dedication to the dishes being created in the open kitchen at the end of the slim dining room. The space is light, bright and airy, belying its square footage but keeping things cosy and intimate.

Every dish you eat has a lightness of touch and an essence of surprise, as the menu doesn't give much away beyond the key ingredients. So, you might order the most glorious piece of fresh monkfish that's accompanied by seaweed; or lamb with goats' curd and artichokes; or Belle de Fontenay potatoes with truffle – but the plate that arrives at the table will be a revelation in presentation.

The dessert menu is equally minimalist but there's no need to worry about not finding something you fancy – it's all wonderful. And when it comes to drinks, you can choose from a selection of cocktails – including house specialities, such as Basil Gin Sour and Portland Old Fashioned – or move straight to the wine list, which is reasonable and extensive.

Mon–Sat 12pm–2:30pm, 6pm–11pm		
Sun Closed	Great Portland Street	88, 453, C2, N18
Opening times	**Tube**	**Bus**

Portland
Challans duck with maple glaze and plum vinegar

SERVES 2–4

1 large Challans duck (or other good French duck)

200 ml (¾ cup) maple syrup

100 ml (½ cup) duck or chicken stock

100 ml (½ cup) plum vinegar or cider vinegar

salt and pepper, to season

At Portland we mostly use French poultry, as I often find it to have better flavour and texture. It is usually fed on a natural diet of grains and seeds and is always free range and slow reared. Sometimes they live up to 130 days before going to the abattoir and this gives them a more interesting flavour. We use mostly Challans ducks at the restaurant but feel free to try other breeds or a good free-range English duck.

Merlin Labron-Johnson, Head Chef

Remove the legs, neck and innards from the duck and pat dry inside and out with a cloth. Reserve the legs for another meal and use the neck and wings for stock. Leave the duck out of the fridge for about 1 hour to come up to room temperature.

Place the maple syrup, stock and vinegar in a small saucepan, season with salt and pepper, bring to a boil and reduce by half. Set aside.

Preheat the oven to 180°C (350°F).

Heat a frying pan large enough to contain the crown of duck. Put the duck in the pan, breast-side down, and reduce the heat (gently applying colour to the breasts will cause the fat to render and make the skin crispy). When the duck is golden all over (about 6 minutes), remove from the pan and place in an oven tray.

Brush the duck all over with the maple syrup glaze and place in the oven for 7 minutes. Remove from the oven and brush again with the glaze. Return to the oven for 8 minutes then remove the duck and leave to rest in a warm place for 10 minutes.

Brush with any remaining glaze. Slice the duck thinly and serve with its juices.

We serve this dish at the restaurant with grilled peaches and fennel salad and we sprinkle chopped toasted pistachios on the skin of the duck. Alternatively, try it with Chinese pancakes, cucumber, spring onion (scallion) and hoi sin.

Taberna do Mercado

Old Spitalfields Market, 107b Commercial Street E1 6BG
+44 (0)20 7375 0649 / www.tabernamercado.co.uk

The food of Portugal has been somewhat underrepresented in the London restaurant scene – being overshadowed by that of its European neighbours. Chefs Nuno Mendes and Antonio Galapito set out to redress the balance when they opened Taberna do Mercado in 2015 with the aim of championing Portuguese recipes and ingredients in their East London restaurant.

Having helped to kickstart the supper club revolution with the Loft Project and then taking the reins in the kitchens at Chiltern Firehouse, Nuno was well placed to put his plan of merging food and ambience into action. While fans of his previous projects rushed to book a table at this simply adorned bistro-style eatery in the heart of Old Spitalfields Market, the easy menu and stylish eating appeals to all manner of diners – from snack-hungry shoppers to those looking to linger over a selection of Portuguese specialities while sipping a glass of Vinho Verde.

The menu is simply divided into snacks, cheese, meat, fish and small plates, with a couple of sandwiches for good measure (though the word hardly does justice to the huge slabs of meat that fill the toasted bread). There's also a selection of incredible desserts which, let's face it, are as much a part of a Portuguese meal as crockery and cutlery.

The food is big but carefully placed; rustic yet elegant; and it takes diners on a crash course of this hearty cuisine that is all about cheese, fish, cured meats, piquant sauces and super-sweet puddings. Try chestnut- or acorn-fed pork, a plate of soft Serra da Estrela cheese, and another of Monkfish Cheeks with Garlic and Shallots. Small plates allow you to sample a grand selection of Portugal's delights – bread pudding, cuttlefish with pig trotters, a stew of lamb sweetbreads. And you can continue with the sharing theme when it comes to dessert with the Olive Oil & Runny Egg Sponge Cake (for two). Naturally, you shouldn't leave without also trying one of the best *pastel de nata* tarts this side of Lisbon.

The wine list is a journey around Portugal's top wineries, including a lovely Tinto from esteemed Casa de Mouraz and the crisp white Aventura produced by award-winning winemaker Susana Esteban.

The buzz of the marketplace echoes the ambience of Lisbon's traditional tabernas, while a small terrace allows for outdoor dining on balmier London evenings. Nuno and Antonio have created a little corner of Lisbon in London and helped to bring Portuguese food to a wider audience in the process.

Mon–Sat 12pm–10pm **Sun** 12pm–3pm, 6pm–8pm	⇌ Shoreditch High Street	 67
Opening times	**Train**	**Bus**

Taberna do Mercado

Abade de priscos

Steamed egg yolk, pork fat & port caramel

SERVES 4–6

For the pudding:

6 organic egg yolks

400 g (2 cups) caster (superfine) sugar

300 ml (1¼ cups) water

3 tbsp diced lardo

1 cinnamon stick

zest of 1 lemon

olive oil, to serve

sea salt, to serve

For the port caramel:

200 g (1 cup) caster (superfine) sugar

100 ml (½ cup) water

50 ml (¼ cup) port

For the port broth:

200 ml (¾ cup) port

100 ml (½ cup) water

2 round orange slices

50 g (¼ cup) caster (superfine) sugar

1 cinnamon stick

Created by keen chef and priest Manuel Joaquim Machado during the nineteenth century, this dish is a speciality of the small Portuguese parish of Priscos, not far from Porto. The rich dessert marries the saltiness of lardo with a sweet port broth.

For the port caramel, add the sugar, water and port to a small pan and bring up to a temperature of 144°C (290°F). Pour into a large pudding mould and move the mould around to cover the base and sides with the caramel. Set aside.

For the pudding, pass the egg yolks through a fine chinois or strainer and reserve.

Place the sugar, water, lardo, cinnamon stick and the lemon zest in a pan and heat to a temperature of exactly 112°C (234°F). Strain the syrup, reserving the liquid.

Very slowly, pour the syrup over the reserved egg yolks, stirring constantly so the mixture doesn't curdle.

Pour the mixture into the mould and set aside to rest for 20 minutes.

Preheat the oven to 100°C (210°F) and place a baking tray containing water inside to create some steam.

Bake the pudding for 20 minutes, until it is soft but not liquid and there is a skin on top.

When cooked, leave the pudding to cool in the mould for 40 minutes before carefully flipping it out onto a serving plate.

Meanwhile, make the port broth. Place the port, water, orange slices, sugar and cinnamon stick in a pan and reduce by half. Remove from the heat, transfer to a bowl or container and leave to cool. Store in the fridge until ready to serve.

Serve a slice of the pudding with a little port broth poured around. Garnish with a drizzle of olive oil and a pinch of sea salt.

Caravan

1 Granary Square N1C 4AA / 30 Great Guildford Street
SE1 0HS / 11–13 Exmouth Market EC1R 4QD
+44 (0)20 7833 8115 / www.caravanrestaurants.co.uk

Caravan is synonymous with the modern dining expectation – a versatile set of menus tailored to a customer base that doesn't want to be told when they should eat. It's a relaxed affair that starts with a leisurely breakfast, followed by an all-day menu, plus brunch at the weekends that allows for serious lie-ins with its 4pm finishing time. But Caravan isn't just about food – they're serious about their coffee too and Caravan Coffee Roasters supplies freshly ground coffee to their own restaurants, plus a growing band of other establishments that appreciate the exceptional quality.

The restaurants were set up by New Zealanders Miles Kirby, Chris Ammermann and Laura Harper-Hinton, the first opening in Exmouth Market in 2010. The fresh interior and plates of globally-inspired food were well received and a second, larger restaurant followed in Granary Square at King's Cross.
With a focus on sharing and a constant influx of diners, you'll find a lively and relaxed atmosphere in both restaurants. A small pizza selection also graces the menu at King's Cross, while coffee obviously plays an important role in both locations.

The roastery is part of the King's Cross restaurant and it's here that the team profiles each batch of beans then roasts and blends them to produce the range of coffees that are brewed and served on site, or sold in the shop.

Each restaurant has seamlessly merged into its surroundings and become both a local favourite and destination diner. The laidback atmosphere combined with memorable food has proved to be a winning combination.

A third site, Caravan Bankside, opened in October 2016.

Mon 8am–10:30pm		
Tues–Fri 8am–11:00pm		
Sat 10am–11pm		
Sun 10am–4pm	Kings Cross	10, 17, 30, 45, 59, 63, 73, 91, 205, 214, 259, 390, 476
Opening times	**Train and Tube**	**Bus**

Caravan

Kimchi pancake, pork belly, duck eggs and gochuchang ketchup

SERVES 4–6

1 duck egg or 2 hens' eggs per person

For the slow cooked pork belly:
1 kg (2 lb) pork belly
1 ltr (4 cups) pork stock

For the kimchi pancake:
1½ tbsp tahini
2 tbsp soy sauce
1 egg
125 ml (½ cup) full-fat milk
1 tbsp rice wine vinegar
150 g (1¼ cups) plain (all-purpose) flour
1 tsp baking powder
250 g (9 oz) roughly chopped kimchi
3 spring onions (scallions), thinly sliced
large bunch coriander (cilantro) leaves,
    roughly chopped
2 tbsp vegetable oil

For the gochuchang ketchup:
125 g (4 oz) gochuchang (Korean fermented
    red chilli bean paste)
50 ml (¼ cup) rice wine vinegar
150 g (1 cup) tahini
75 ml (⅓ cup) sesame oil
50 ml (¼ cup) soy sauce
75 g (⅓ cup) caster (superfine) sugar
3 tbsp confit garlic purée

Kimchi is a traditional Korean dish of preserved vegetables and chillies that is served as a condiment or side dish. Piquant kimchi pancakes are the perfect complement for rich, fat-laden pork belly.

Slow-cooked pork belly
Use a sharp knife to score the skin of the pork belly at 1-cm (½-inch) intervals. Place in a large pan or dish and cover in brine (1 litre/4 cups of water to 100 g/½ cup fine sea salt). Leave overnight in the fridge.

Preheat the oven to 160°C (325°F). Bring the stock to the boil in a large pan.

Remove the pork from the brine and place in a deep roasting tray. Pour over the stock and cover with parchment paper, then seal with foil. Cook the pork for 3½ hours, or until the meat pulls apart easily.

Carefully remove the pork from the roasting tray and place on a chopping board. Slice off the skin. Allow to rest then carve into long slices before serving.

Kimchi pancake
Preheat the oven to 180°C (350°F).

Whisk the tahini, soy sauce, egg, milk and vinegar together in a medium bowl.

Sift the flour and baking powder into the bowl and stir to form a batter. Add the kimchi, spring onion (scallion) and coriander (cilantro) and stir.

Heat the vegetable oil in a heavy-based 20-cm (8-in) skillet or pan and add the mixture. Cook on one side on the hob for a few minutes then place in the oven for 15 minutes.

Remove from the oven, flip the pancake and return to the oven for a further 5 minutes.

When the pancake is ready, remove from the oven and turn out onto a board. Cut into 8–12 pieces.

Gochuchang ketchup
Place all the ingredients in a bowl and whisk together. Let it stand for the sugar to dissolve and the garlic to impart its flavour. This will keep in an airtight container in the fridge for up to 3 weeks.

Bringing the dish together
Cook the pancake while the pork is resting. When the pancake is cooked, leave to rest and carve the pork, then cut up the pancake.

Fry 1 duck egg or 2 hens' eggs per person. Assemble all the ingredients on serving plates and top with the gochuchang ketchup.

Barrafina

10 Adelaide Street WC2N 4HZ / 54 Frith Street W1D 4SL/ 43 Drury Lane WC2B 5AJ
www.barrafina.co.uk

London fell in love with Spanish tapas a long time ago (and, more recently, small-plate and tapas-style food from all manner of cuisines – think Polpo and Imli Street) and it's easy to see why: as we grin and bear our interminable and unpredictable weather, hopping inside a tapas bar is like being instantly transported to a sunny Spanish plaza. These restaurants are usually frenetic, fun and ooze the fragrant aromas of the Med – and the cosy interiors of the Barrafina restaurants are no exception.

Founded by brothers Sam and Eddie Hart, who wanted to recreate a little bit of Barcelona in central London, the first restaurant opened on Frith Street in 2007 – and, after remaining a sole venture for seven years, two more tapas bars followed in quick succession on Adelaide Street and Drury Lane.

Once you have – probably – queued and secured a seat at the bar (there are no reservations at Barrafina) you'll be greeted by the chatter of chefs working in the open kitchens. As well as creating that all-important atmosphere, the laid-bare kitchens act as an aromatic aperitif with the smell of sizzling garlic, meat and the speciality seafood dishes, making short shrift of the ordering process.

Daily specials complement the menus and each small plate is a treasure trove of gorgeous ingredients – delicate courgette flowers, octopus, little fillets of fried fish, salt cod and pork belly to name a few. You can accompany the food with a glass or two of sherry or cava for an authentic Spanish tapas experience, which means you can either pop in for a few post-work or pre-dinner nibbles over drinks, or order more fervently for a full meal. However, for most people, the hour-long queue means settling in for a proper tasting session and cancelling any subsequent plans.

Opening times	Tube	Bus
Mon–Sat 12pm–3pm, 5pm–11pm **Sun** 1pm–3:30pm, 5:30pm–10pm	Leicester Square	14, 19, 38, N19, N38

Barrafina
Stuffed courgette flowers

SERVES 5 as a starter (10 as a tapas)

10 courgette (zucchini) flowers

300 g (10½ oz) goat's cheese
  (preferably Spanish)

2 tsp thyme leaves

175 g (1½ cups) plain (all-purpose) flour

500 ml (2 cups) water

vegetable oil, for deep-frying

100 ml (⅓ cup) orange blossom honey

Malden sea salt and freshly ground pepper,
  to season

A favourite among visitors, this dish is a Barrafina staple and one that you will find on the menu across all three restaurants. Stuffed with goat's cheese and fried in an extra light batter, these delicate flowers make a perfect starter or simple tapa. Use Spanish goat's cheese, if possible – Mont Enebro is a good choice.

Check that the flowers are clean. In a small bowl, mix the goat's cheese with the thyme and pepper, to taste. Carefully stuff the flowers with this mixture, wrapping the petals around the stuffing to keep it in place.

Sift the flour into a mixing bowl and gradually whisk in the water to make a light batter. Heat the oil in a suitable pan to 180°C (350°F). Dip the stuffed flowers, a few at a time, into the batter to coat and then immerse in the hot oil. Deep-fry for 3 minutes until crisp and golden.

Remove with a slotted spoon and drain on kitchen paper. Sprinkle with sea salt then lightly drizzle the orange blossom honey over the flowers and serve immediately.

Craft London

Peninsula Square, Greenwich Peninsula SE10 0SQ
+44 (0)20 8465 5910 / www.craft-london.co.uk

Stevie Parle and Tom Dixon have brought some serious restaurant kudos to an often-overlooked part of South-east London. In the process, they have satisfied the palates of a discerning bunch of local diners who now have fine dining on their doorsteps.

As a pioneer of the pop-up movement, Stevie went on to launch Dock Kitchen in 2009 – a permanent base for his creative talents. The restaurant is located in designer Tom Dixon's studio, so it seemed like a small leap for the pair to work together on a new venture that would combine high-end food with impeccable design. The result is Craft London: a three-storey standalone bar, restaurant and café that sits just next to the O2 in North Greenwich.

The restaurant is in the middle of the building and it's here that you can sample Stevie's unique take on modern British cuisine, with seasonal flavours taking precedence on a menu that includes the signature clay-baked duck, as well as Cornish cod, Devon beef sirloin and Craft cotechino. This last ingredient – cured meat similar to salami – is produced on site, as are the honey and butter that are used across the menu; nearly everything else is sourced from quality British producers.

Upstairs in the bar you can appreciate Tom Dixon's stunning design, enjoy 360-degree views across town and, on warmer evenings, have your drinks served on the terrace. Choose from a selection of craft lagers and ales, or cocktails from a list created by Adam Wyatt-Jones, whose bartending credentials include heading up the team at Milk & Honey.

The ground-floor café is a welcome addition to the limited caffeine options previously available to local workers, residents and visitors. Homemade bread, fresh salads, cakes and pastries are always available and the coffee is roasted on site. Sit outside and you can wander into the three-acre Alys Fowler-designed Peninsula Garden – home to the annual Urban Village Fete.

Tue–Fri 5:30pm–10:30pm
Sat 1pm–3:30pm, 5:30pm–10:30pm
Sun–Mon Closed

North Greenwich

161, 472, 108, 422, 186

Opening times (restaurant)

Tube

Bus

Craft London

More please

50 ml (3 tbsp) gin
15 ml (1 tbsp) camomile flower-infused apricot liqueur
15ml (1 tbsp) London Honey Syrup
20ml (4 tsp) lemon juice
20ml (4 tsp) egg white
3 dried camomile flowers, to decorate

Working with flowers is the same for me as any ingredient – freshness is paramount, as that's when you get the most flavour. I believe you should be able to taste every ingredient in a drink, otherwise it has no place. With flowers that's sometimes hard but I've found drying them – as in this recipe – or pickling them, as we have done with rose petals, can amplify the natural notes. During the summer months I like to create light yet flavoursome drinks that utilise seasonal ingredients. Flowers are another way of creating exciting combinations that especially fit with what we're doing at Craft London.

**Adam Wyatt-Jones,
Head Bartender**

Combine all the ingredients in a cocktail shaker.

First it is dry shaken, then wet shaken and single-strained into the coupette (specifically a 'Speakeasy Cocktail Coup').

Finally, decorate with 3 dried camomile flowers.

Quince gimlet

35 ml (2 tbsp) Plymouth gin
40 ml (3 tbsp) bramley and gage quince cordial (or Rose's lime cordial)
2 dashes absinthe

Originally an officer's drink in the mid 1800s to ensure sailors took their daily ration of lime, this twist on a gimlet brings Greenwich's rich naval history to Craft London. The classic uses Rose's lime cordial, which here has been replaced by a house-made bramley apple and gage quince cordial (you can make this delicious cordial at home or feel free to use the original Rose's for an equally delicious drink).

Use a cocktail-stirring glass or shaker with as much ice in as possible. Pour in the gin and cordial and stir 10 times before leaving for 30 seconds to cool and dilute.

Add 2 dashes of a good-quality absinthe and then strain into a coupette. If you're making your own cordial, start with 30 ml (2 tbsp) and add more if the drink isn't balanced.

The Modern Pantry

17 18 St John's Square EC1V 4JJ / The Alphabeta Building, 14 Finsbury Square EC2A 1AH
+44 (0)20 7553 9210 / +44 (0)20 3696 6565 / www.themodernpantry.co.uk

When The Modern Pantry first opened its doors in 2008 it was a breath of fresh air, with its eclectic menu that fused global ingredients into a melting pot of dishes that offered punchy flavours with a delicate touch.

Spread over three floors in a stunning Georgian townhouse in Clerkenwell, The Modern Pantry encompasses a laid-back ground floor café and bar, the first floor restaurant, and a private dining room at the top of the house, where diners can enjoy the restaurant's fairly priced set menus in a more intimate space.

Once success was sealed, the Clerkenwell restaurant was joined by a sister establishment just down the road in Finsbury Square in 2015, where the same fusion-style cookery was put in place, although also available in smaller portions – this restaurant serves tapas in the bar area, while a full menu is available in the impressive dining room.

Back to Clerkenwell, where chef and founder Anna Hansen has carved out a niche for her unique style of cooking and flavour combinations. Having worked with Fergus Henderson (St. John) and Peter Gordon (Anna and Peter launched The Providores), Anna used her skills and experience to further develop her interpretation of contemporary ingredients. At The Modern Pantry, pork chops share plate space with ras el hanout and parsley root mash; while onglet steak is marinated in miso and tamarind and served with cassava chips. And if you've never tried garam masala ice cream, now's your opportunity.

While less-confident chefs would shy away from pushing the boundaries of diners' palates by marrying such diverse ingredients, Anna creates exciting dishes with a global provenance that is sophisticated rather than showy – it's all there for a reason. The critics agree and the restaurant has 2 AA rosettes as well as a Bib Gourmand in the Michelin Guide 2009 and 2010.

Mon Closed
Tue–Fri 12pm–3pm, 6pm–10:30pm
Sat 9am–4pm, 6pm–10:30pm
Sun 10am–4pm

Farringdon

153, 55, 243, N55

**Opening times
(restaurant)**

Train and Tube

Bus

Pitt Cue Co.

1 The Avenue, Devonshire Square EC2M 4YP / 1 Newburgh Street W1F 7RB
+44 (0)20 7324 7770 / www.pittcue.co.uk

From a Southbank food van serving meat boxes and burgers to a celebrated City restaurant – via a basement in Soho – Pitt Cue has travelled a long way in the last few years. The robust barbecue dining experience celebrates meat in all its glory and makes little excuse for those who prefer a less carnivorous evening out.

The menu has grown up and expanded, along with the venue – a bigger kitchen means head chef and co-founder Tom Adams can fully indulge his passion for barbecuing, smoking and sourcing the best meat on the market. That includes the rare breed Mangalitza pigs that are a star feature on the menu and are raised in Cornwall in a joint venture between Tom and a local farmer.

Provenance is key to the ethos of Pitt Cue and every last morsel on the compact menu is carefully considered. The main meat section – which includes onglet and featherblade steaks, shortrib, and Mangalitza chop – is where most diners focus their attention but the bar snacks and starters shouldn't be overlooked: Octopus and Whey, Pig's Head Scrumpet, and Salt Beef and Gherkin all prove worthy prologues to the main event. A selection of sides and puddings challenges those with truly hearty appetites, while the drinks menu embraces the American barbecue theme with classic cocktails, rye, bourbon and rum sharing space with a great range of craft lagers and ales, and an impressive wine list that was introduced when Pitt Cue parked its smoker in City territory.

The interior combines industrial chic with stainless steel, leather and wood to create a fitting cocoon in which to wallow in unadulterated barbecue heaven, with big flavours that celebrate the best cuts and varieties of meat cooked long and slow or fast and furious over flames or smoke.

With the recently opened Little Pitt now offering a pared-down version of the full menu back in the restaurant's original location in Soho, visitors to the centre and the City of London can all enjoy barbecue heaven.

Mon–Fri 12pm–3pm, 6pm–10:30pm		
Sat 6pm–10:30pm		
Sun Closed	Aldgate	15, 25, 40, 67, 78, 100
Opening times	**Tube**	**Bus**

BAO

53 Lexington Street W1F 9AS / 31 Windmill Street W1T 2JN
no reservations / www.baolondon.com

Bao means 'bun' and that's the highlight of a visit to this compact café-style, no-bookings restaurant on Soho's Lexington Street. If there was any doubt as to the quality of what lies within, just check out the queue (chances are there'll be one whatever time of day you turn up).

What began as a Taiwanese street food pop-up (the original BAO Bar recently reopened in Netil Market, E8) has landed on its permanent feet in an area that craves this style of innovative fast food and is happy to patiently wait for something more interesting for lunch than a cardboard sandwich. The soft, fluffy milk buns are steamed and the classic variety is filled with braised pork then topped with peanut powder and coriander.

If you've got a bit more time and can manage to do the almost impossible and secure a table or bar stool, you can supplement your pork buns with other varieties – fillings include fried chicken, lamb shoulder and daikon – as well as a number of small plates, and make a meal of it.

The menu is compact but perfectly formed and means you can try a good selection of everything on offer in one sitting. Don't let dishes like Pig Blood Cake or Trotter Nuggets restrict your choices – both are delicious; the no-frills descriptions are just part of the minimalist style. The 40-day Rump Cap with Aged White Soy Sauce is the most expensive item on the menu but still incredible value for the quality on the plate. You can easily fill yourself up here for under a tenner but make sure you leave room for the solitary sweet dish on the menu – Fried Horlicks Ice Cream Bao. I won't spoil it by revealing exactly what this small round of deliciousness entails but don't leave without trying one.

BAO proved such a success with the Soho set that the team opened a second, larger site on Windmill Street in nearby Fitzrovia that features a different menu but the same relaxed dining experience.

Mon–Fri 12pm–3pm, 5:30pm–10pm
Sat 12pm–10pm
Sun Closed

Piccadilly Circus

12, 88, 94, 159, N3

Opening times

Tube

Bus

Ottolenghi

287 Upper Street N1 2TZ / 63 Ledbury Road W11 2AD / 13 Motcomb
Street SW1X 8LB / 50 Artillery Lane E1 7LJ / NOPI 21–22 Warwick
Street W1B 5NE +44 (0)20 7288 1454 / www.ottolenghi.co.uk

Israeli-born chef and food writer Yotam Ottolenghi propelled high-quality vegetarian cuisine onto the mainstream London dining scene at a time when carnivores still shied away from the idea of a meal without meat.

Although not vegetarian by any means, Yotam's food does shine a long overdue beacon of light on fruit, vegetables and pulses, with aromatic herbs and fragrant spices elevating every dish. Ottolenghi delis are known for their glorious displays of freshly prepared salads, roasted vegetables, quiches, dips and fritters (as well as bread, cakes and pastries) that stop passersby in their tracks and turn the traditional notion of vegetarian fare on its head, give it a good shake and showcase it in technicolour splendour.

Having earned his stripes working as a pastry chef at some of London's top kitchens (including Launceston Place), Yotam teamed up with fellow chef Sami Tamimi, and entrepreneur Noam Bar to set up the first Ottolenghi deli in Notting Hill in 2002. With a tiny seating area, the deli relied on people embracing this fresh approach to the salad counter but embrace it they did and more openings followed in Islington, Belgravia and, most recently, Spitalfields. The Islington branch bridged the gap between deli and restaurant, with plenty of tables, as well as a lunch and dinner menu – though the trademark take-out counter still steals the limelight.

In between launching these hugely successful delis, the team took the leap to the full restaurant concept and NOPI opened in Soho in 2011. Although the menu is based on Yotam's trademark bold flavours, there is a distinction here between communal dining in the downstairs room – where you can watch chefs at work in the open kitchen – and the more formal set-up upstairs.

Aside from recipe development, cookbooks, television appearances and regular newspaper columns, Yotam remains very hands-on and is involved in the day-to-day running of all the delis and the restaurant. His food is a culinary stream of consciousness that involves constant experimention with flavour and ingredient combinations.

Mon–Sat 8am–10:30pm		
Sun 9am–7pm	Angel	19, 38, N19, N38, N41
Opening times	**Tube**	**Bus**

THE SCHOOL OF ST. JOHN

It is a truly accomplished eatery that deserves its own chapter in a book. However, the contribution to the London food scene that has been made by maverick restaurateurs Fergus Henderson and Trevor Gulliver cannot be underestimated.

Following separate, diverse and independently successful careers in food, Fergus and Trevor's paths crossed, friendship blossomed and the idea of a joint venture came to fruition in the form of St. John. That was over 20 years ago and, in the intervening period, the duo has – without any hint of exaggeration – transformed London's restaurant landscape.

From opening subsequent joint ventures and shaking up long-held assumptions about what diners want to eat – and are willing to try – to nurturing and training a whole generation of likeminded chefs and restaurateurs who have taken on board the ethos of St. John and followed it through to their own unique conclusion, Fergus and Trevor's influence has been monumental.

The knock-on effect of their staunch focus on British ingredients and reintroducing parts of the animal to the menu that had lost favour with diners has been felt in restaurants not only in the capital but also around the world. In fact, Fergus personally shares his nose-to-tail eating philosophy with New York diners in his annual FergusStock festival. This sees him team up with fellow chef (and expat Brit) April Bloomfield to prepare some of his key dishes at her highly regarded restaurants the Spotted Pig, The Breslin Bar & Dining Room and The John Dory Oyster Bar.

This chapter celebrates the achievements of St. John, as well as restaurants founded on its principles by those who worked alongside the duo, or trained in their kitchens.

St. John

26 St. John Street EC1M 4AY / 94–96 Commercial Street E1 6LZ / 41 Maltby Street SE1 3PA / +44 (0)20 7251 0848 / www.stjohngroup.uk.com

If one restaurant sums up London's food evolution and its positive engagement in its culinary past, present and future, it has to be St. John. An unassuming frontage gives way to a fresh, modern interior where founders Fergus Henderson and Trevor Gulliver began the nose-to-tail eating revolution when they opened the restaurant in 1994.

From the outset, the focus was on rustic fare that harked back to a more prudent approach to butchery and food preparation. Not exactly thrifty – more respectful of the whole animal – this nod to traditional meat eating initially caused a stir. But it was soon embraced and emulated, as people began to understand the philosophy behind the menu and, having eaten at the restaurant, appreciated how ordering organs and entrails could broaden their culinary horizons.

The menu is a movable daily feast that is only set in stone shortly before service begins and diners could be enjoying delights such as crispy pig skin, tripe, liver or ox cheek. The chefs also tweak as they go, adding dishes that might evolve in the kitchen during prep, depending on what goodies have been delivered from suppliers that day.

This relaxed and flexible attitude spills over to the business as a whole and Fergus, Trevor and their team have their fingers in many pies. This has very much been an organic expansion that has seen the opening of St. John Bread and Wine in Spitalfields, as well as a bakery on Druid Street, which in turn led to the opening of the delightful St. John Maltby Street.

Each venue is unique but there's a very distinct style – from food to décor – that gathers all branches of the business under the St. John umbrella. Fergus and Trevor remain very involved in the day-to-day running of the restaurants and who knows where their successful collaboration will take them next in the capital.

Mon–Fri 12pm–3pm, 6pm–11pm		
Sat 6pm–11pm		
Sun 12:30pm–4pm	Farringdon	4, 56, 153
Opening times	**Train and Tube**	Bus

TO BAR AND DINING ROOM →

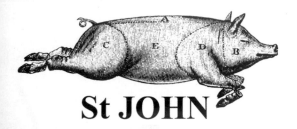

St JOHN

St. John
Snail, trotter, sausage and chickpeas

SERVES 8

400 g (2 cups) dried chickpeas, soaked in
    cold water overnight
2 heads of garlic
12 shallots, peeled and left whole
splash of olive oil
handful of green bacon chunks
12 cloves of garlic, peeled and left whole
500 g (1 lb) Trotter Gear (see below)
bundle thyme, rosemary and parsley stalks
10 small chorizo sausages
40 fresh snails
2 bunches of rocket
sea salt and freshly ground black pepper

For the vinaigrette:
1 tsp Dijon mustard
2 tbsp red wine vinegar
75 ml (⅓ cup) olive oil

For the Trotter Gear:
6 pigs' trotters
2 onions, peeled
2 carrots, peeled
2 sticks of celery
2 leeks, slit in half lengthways and cleaned
1 head of garlic
bundle of thyme
handful of black peppercorns
56 bottle of Sercial Madeira
sufficient chicken stock to cover the trotters

This is the epitome of comfort food – an unctuous garlicky sauce spiked with chunky chorizo and a generous helping of Trotter Gear. Fresh snails are gently simmered and the whole is topped with rocket (a pile, not a garnish).

Drain the chickpeas, cover with fresh water in a large pan and add the heads of garlic. Bring to the boil then cook at a gentle simmer for about 3 hours (the chickpeas should be soft and giving).

In a large ovenproof casserole, gently brown the shallots in the oil, then add the bacon. Allow to sizzle then add the garlic cloves, Trotter Gear (see recipe below), herbs and chorizo sausages. Add the chickpeas, using a slotted spoon. Add a little chickpea juice to achieve a sauce consistency.

Simmer for 20 minutes, then remove the chorizo and season the sauce to taste.

Preheat the oven to 200°C (400°F). Chop the chorizo into finger-width slices and return to the chickpeas. Add the snails, stir and cover the pan. Bake in the oven for 35 minutes.

Roughly chop the rocket. Combine all the ingredients for the vinaigrette and dress the rocket. Divide the snails, sausage and chickpeas between serving bowls and top with rocket.

Trotter Gear
Place the trotters in a large casserole. Cover with water and bring to the boil. Boil for 5 minutes then drain.

Return the blanched trotters to the casserole, add the vegetables, garlic, thyme, peppercorns and Madeira and cover with stock. Cook for at least 3 hours, until the trotters are totally giving. Strain the cooking liquor and reserve.

When the trotters are cool enough to handle, pick all the flesh, fat and skin off them, tearing the skin into shreds. Add to the cooking liquor, seal in a jar and refrigerate.

St. John
Roast bone marrow and parsley salad

SERVES 3–4

12 x 7–8 cm (3-in) pieces middle veal
   bone marrow
large bunch of flat parsley, leaves picked
2 shallots, peeled and very thinly sliced
small handful of capers (extra fine,
   if possible)
good supply of toast

For the dressing:
juice of 1 lemon
extra virgin olive oil
pinch of salt and pepper
coarse sea salt

This is one dish that never changes on the menu at St. John. The ends of the bone marrow are often covered so the marrow doesn't escape but I prefer to see some colour and crispiness so I leave them uncovered. You'll need teaspoons to scrape the marrow out of the bone.

Preheat the oven to 250°C (480°F).

Put the bone marrow in an ovenproof frying pan and roast for about 20 minutes, depending on the thickness of the bone. The marrow should be loose and giving but not melted away.

Meanwhile, prepare the dressing by combining all the ingredients in a bowl and mixing well.

Combine the parsley, shallots and capers and mix lightly with the dressing.

Arrange the bone marrow on serving plates and accompany with a handful of dressed leaves. Serve with toast.

Hereford Road

3 Hereford Road W2 4AB
+44 (0)20 7727 1144 / www.herefordroad.org

Occupying what was a Victorian butcher's shop in a leafy street just off Westbourne Grove, Hereford Road's no-nonsense British approach in the kitchen is still as rare in this tract of west London as it was when it opened back in 2007. The natural habitat for this sort of gutsy cooking is still east London and sadly not the borders of Bayswater and Notting Hill.

Accordingly, Hereford Road is the unofficial West London chapter of St. John – its driving force, chef-proprietor Tom Pemberton, previously ran the kitchen at St. John Bread & Wine. He must take the occasional day off but regulars might beg to differ, as he always seems to be behind the stove in its open kitchen, located at the entrance to the restaurant and framed by the large window of its old shop front.

There's wrought ironwork on the ceiling and red leather upholstered loveseats at the front overlooking the kitchen, while at the back of the room things are more light and spacious with booths and tables overlooked by a large central skylight.

The daily changing menu delivers delicious seasonal simplicity with everything from grilled whole fish and sharing dishes – such as legs of lamb and shoulders of venison – to game birds, plates of offal, rib-sticking puddings and perfect sorbets. The menu always reflects seasonality but no matter the time of year, will always leave you spoilt for choice. Its set lunch menu remains a true bargain in a city where cooking this accomplished rarely costs so little.

A regular fixture on that set menu is this crispy pork dish with chicory and mustard.

Opening times	Tube	Bus
Mon–Sat 12pm–3pm, 6pm–10:30pm	Bayswater	7, 27, 28, 31, 328, N28
Sun 12pm–4pm, 6pm–10pm		

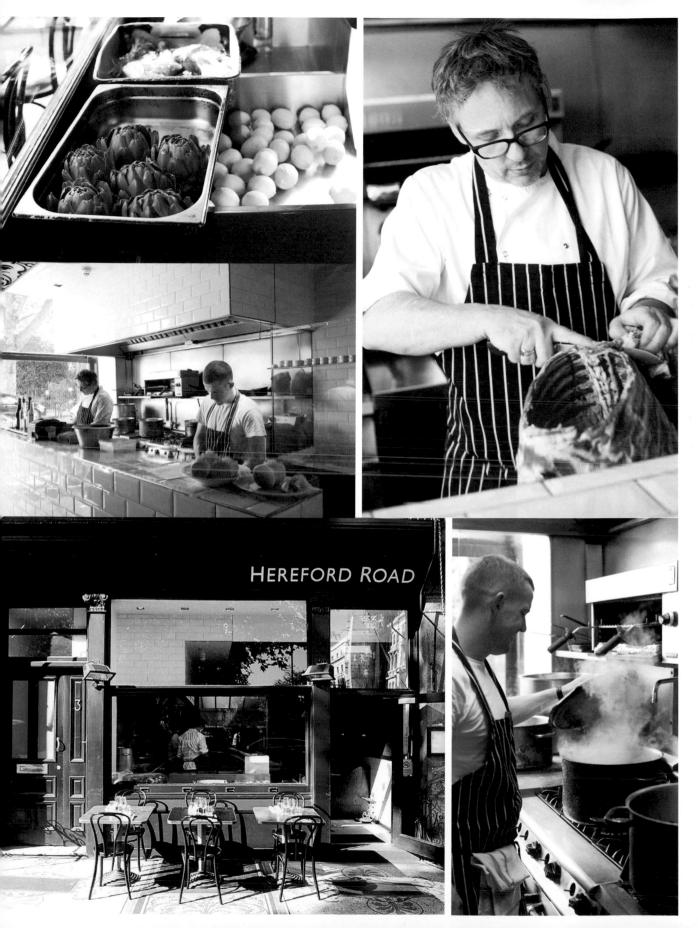

Crispy pork, chicory & mustard

SERVES 4

1 medium pork belly (Middle White
or other outdoor-reared breed)
60 ml (¼ cup) vegetable oil
2 tbsp butter
juice of ½ lemon
salt and pepper, to season

For the pickled turnips:
(optional addition to the salad)
20 small-medium turnips
1 ltr (4 cups) white wine vinegar
500 g (2½ cups) caster (superfine) sugar
1 star anise
1 mild red chilli
6 cloves
10-cm (4-in) piece fresh ginger, peeled
and chopped
salt, to season

Crisping the belly:
cooked pork belly
vegetable oil, for frying
1 tbsp sherry vinegar
salt and pepper, to season

For the salad:
1 head chicory (Belgian endive), leaves
separated
1 bunch dandelion leaves
200 g (7 oz) rocket (arugula)
1 bunch watercress
1 bunch English breakfast radishes
with tops, sliced into quarters
1 tbsp chopped cornichons
1 tsp capers
3 spring onions (scallions), sliced

For the vinaigrette:
1 garlic clove, finely chopped
3 tbsp Dijon mustard
3 tbsp red wine vinegar
250 ml (1 cup) olive oil

Tom Pemberton's recipe combines saltiness, sweetness, sourness and bitterness. It is the ratio of meat to fat and the surface area of the skin that makes belly the best cut: choose a quality breed like Middle White.

Pickled turnips (prepare 4 days in advance)
Peel and quarter the turnips and very lightly salt.

Make the pickling solution by adding the white wine vinegar, sugar, star anise, red chilli, cloves and ginger to a large pan. Bring to the boil and simmer for a few minutes. Allow to cool.

Wash the salt off the turnips and pat dry. Place in a sterile container and pour over the cooled vinegar. Leave for at least 4 days.

Cooking the belly
Allow the pork to come to room temperature. Slash the skin across the surface to a depth of 2 mm (⅔ inch) (a Stanley knife is great for this).

Rub the vegetable oil, butter, lemon juice, salt and pepper into the skin. Place a wire rack over a roasting tray and put the pork on this. Place a metal tray under the pork so the fat runs off.

Preheat the oven to 250°C (480°F). Cook the pork for 30 minutes, until the skin is crisp. Reduce the temperature to 170°C (325°F) and cook for a further 2 hours. Remove from the oven and cool before placing in the fridge.

Crisping the belly
Cut the belly into cubes approximately 5 x 5 cm (2 x 2 in).

Heat a little vegetable oil in a thick-based, ovenproof frying pan. Add the pork when the oil is hot and season well with salt and pepper. Allow the pork to caramelise on each side.

Place the pan in the oven for 7–8 minutes.

Salad
In a bowl, combine the salad leaves and radishes with the cornichons, capers, sliced pickled turnips (optional) and spring onions (scallions).

To make the vinaigrette, add the garlic, mustard and vinegar to a food processor and slowly add the oil so it emulsifies.

Dress the salad with the vinaigrete. Remove the crispy pork from the oven, add to the salad, along with a little fat, and toss through to combine.

Lyle's

Tea Building, 56 Shoreditch High Street E1 6JJ
+44 (0)20 3011 5911 / www.lyleslondon.com

A partnership between front-of-house John Ogier and chef James Lowe, Lyle's opened in
April 2014 in Shoreditch's Tea Building which, as the name suggests, used to store tea. Lowe
was head chef at St. John Bread & Wine before founding the Young Turks with Isaac McHale,
who now runs the Clove Club (page 114) in nearby Old Street.

St. John is an obvious influence, particularly in terms of the stripped-back spartan interior
– a whitewashed warehouse with a high ceiling, industrial pendant lights, commanding
open kitchen and bare tables. Flooded with natural light during the day, it's a calm,
civilised space, which is partly down to the sound-absorbing panels fitted to the ceiling to
soften the sound bouncing off all of those hard surfaces.

When it comes to the daily changing menu, the love and appreciation of top-quality
ingredients is apparent, as well as the attention to detail in the equisitite presentation of
each dish. Lowe is a champion of seasonal British produce with an emphasis on making
use of the whole beast – using less glamorous cuts and offal – and a love of game. However,
he also has a soft spot for vegetables and employs modern techniques, alongside unfussy but
pretty presentation that are very much his own trademarks. He's also turned his restaurant
into a hub of creativity and cooperation, working with likeminded cooks from around the
world and hosting a series of special events featuring guest chefs.

Lyle's is open all day during the week and features an a la carte lunch, followed by dinner,
which is a no-choice four-course affair with a few snacks and treats thrown in. Both offer
remarkably good value for the standard of cooking on offer – the restaurant is a recent
recipient of a Michelin star. The wine list leans towards the interesting and natural and –
like everything else served – the coffee is exceptional.

Lyle's take their food seriously but you don't have to look too hard to see the love that goes
into everything they do. After all, Lowe named the restaurant after his grandmother.

Mon–Fri 8am–11pm		
Sat 12pm–11pm		
Sun Closed	Shoreditch High Street	8, 388, N8
Opening times	**Train**	**Bus**

Lyle's
Fish head

SERVES 1

1 fish head (turbot, brill or cod)

2 ltr (8 cups) water

75 g (¼ cup) sea salt

150 g (1¼ sticks) butter

200 ml (¾ cup) fish stock

juice of 1 lemon

1 lobe of bottarga (salted, cured fish roe)

One of the most incredible things I've ever eaten was in Shanghai – 'deep sea fish head cooked in scallions'. There was so much gelatin in the meat and skin and it was a real thrill to eat; the flavour was so different to that of a bone-free roast fillet. I felt privileged to have been able to eat it and thought that, aside from people being a bit squeamish initially, everyone would enjoy the texture and flavour.

The food at Lyle's isn't the cheapest in London but it is certainly one of the best-value menus. One of the ways we make the most of an expensive fish such as turbot is by not throwing a single part away. We generally brine and age the body but we serve the heads straight away, either on the lunch menu or as an optional extra on the dinner menu.

We either skewer the head and cook it over the grill or roast it in our wood-fired oven. This has a very special effect on the skin due to the intense, dry heat and flavour of the oven.

Co-founder and Head Chef, James Lowe

The day before: rinse the fish head and remove the gills and any blood lines from inside the head.

Make the brine by heating the water slightly in a large pan and whisking in the salt until dissolved. Chill to fridge temperature.

Once the brine is cold, submerge the head and leave overnight.

Take the head from the brine the following day. Preheat the oven to 210°C (410°F).

Place the head on a 5-cm (2-in) deep baking tray lined with baking parchment, or in a casserole. Add the butter and place in the oven.

Baste the head with the butter every 3–4 minutes. After 12 minutes add the fish stock to deglaze the pan.

Unlike cooking a fillet, don't worry about overcooking the head. It needs to cook through to get the most from the gelatinous pieces.

Baste the head with the stock. After 20 minutes take out the head. Squeeze the lemon juice over and set aside to rest.

Once cooled a little, you can serve. Taste the juices around the head; they should be salty, acidic and rich. If any of those are lacking, add more salt, lemon juice or butter.

Transfer to a plate and pour over the cooking juices. Grate bottarga over the whole plate with a fine microplane.

Rochelle Canteen

Rochelle School, Arnold Circus E2 7ES
+44 (0)20 7729 5677 / www.arnoldandhenderson.com

Rochelle School is no longer a school; it's an artists' enclave in the heart of achingly hip Shoreditch. But when it was still a place of learning, the space that is now occupied by Rochelle Canteen served as the bike shed. That was until Margot Henderson and Melanie Arnold moved in to set up a kitchen for their successful catering company Arnold & Henderson.

As they served lunches to the appreciative artists, word spread and the public made a beeline to get a taste of their no-nonsense meals – a selection of daily updated dishes that take the best of British ingredients and plate them up in generous portions.

Open daily for breakfast, lunch and tea (there's no dinner service), this is a canteen in more than just name. It's a far cry from Margot's past life working alongside her husband Fergus Henderson at the French House Dining Room, before he left to set up St. John. The gleaming white walls, vaulted ceiling and wipe-clean tables – devoid of linen or fussy place settings – definitely make the interior more café than restaurant looks wise, but then that was always the idea. ornate place settings, mood lighting and music are set aside for the catering branch of the business

Rochelle Canteen is tucked away to such an extent that passersby are often blissfully unaware of the culinary magic that takes place behind the unmarked entrance. But once discovered, you'll have the lunch of your life with the likes of brill, grilled lamb, beef cheeks and seasonal vegetables making regular appearances on the menu. However, if you want to toast your good fortune at finding this gem with a glass of wine, you'll need to bring your own and pay a small corkage: Rochelle Canteen is all about the food.

Mon–Fri 9am–4:30pm	⇌	
Sat–Sun Closed	Shoreditch High Street	8, 388, N8
Opening times	**Train**	**Bus**

Rochelle Canteen
Braised shoulder of lamb, shallots and flageolet beans

SERVES 6–8

125 ml (½ cup) olive oil

2 kg (4½ lb) shallots, peeled

2 heads garlic, peeled

3 stalks celery, sliced

4 fennel bulbs, sliced

1 bundle of herbs (thyme, bay leaves,
  rosemary), tied up in cooking twine

375 ml (1½ cups) red wine

1 ltr (4 cups) chicken stock

1 x shoulder of lamb (about 2 kg/4½ lb)

500 g (2½ cups) flageolet beans, soaked
  overnight and cooked until tender

2 bags watercress

salt and freshly ground black pepper,
  to season

This dish can be cooked the day before and then reheated. You could make a hearty lamb and bean broth with any leftovers; just add some kale or sprout tops.

Preheat the oven to 180°C (350°F).

Heat the olive oil in a large pan, add the shallots, garlic, celery and fennel and gently brown.

Add the herbs. When the shallots start to brown, add the wine and chicken stock.

Pour the vegetables into a large oven tray and place the lamb on top. Season with salt and pepper and cover with kitchen foil.

Place in the oven, reduce the heat to 150°C (300°F) and cook for 2 hours.

Add the cooked flageolet beans (drained) and cook for 1 hour.

Remove the foil and cook for another 30 minutes to brown the meat.

Just before serving, add the watercress to the pan and allow to wilt into the juices. Check the seasoning. The meat should be beautiful and tender and should fall away easily. You can serve with green sauce (salsa verde) or aioli and a watercress salad.

The Marksman

254 Hackney Road E2 7SJ
+44 (0)20 7739 7393 / www.marksmanpublichouse.com

When Tom Harris and Jon Rotheram headed up the kitchen of the former St. John Hotel as head chef and sous chef respectively, the restaurant gained a Michelin star. So, at first glance, an East End pub might not appear to be the best outlet for their incredible talents. But this isn't any old London boozer; it's a public house and dining room of the highest order, serving quality ales, lagers and stouts, exceptional food, and booting the term 'gastropub' to the outer hemisphere in the process.

The interior was sensitively refurbished before The Marksman opened in 2015. Downstairs the dark wood panelling, leather banquette seating and traditional bar is warm and inviting. Upstairs the duo have teamed up with London-based Italian designer Martino Gamper to create a light, airy room that is modern but still manages to connect to the rest of the building.

The menus change daily to keep the regulars on their toes but there's always a selection of small, medium and larger plates that take the best of British ingredients and rework classic dishes for the modern mealtime. The Beef & Barley Bun is a popular choice, but you could also be tucking into Salted Hake Rissoles, Cured Ham with Pickles, and Brown Butter & Honey Tart.

As this part of town continues to gentrify, there's no shortage of locals looking for upmarket food and drink with the added bonus of a genuine pub atmosphere. The Marksman is a popular addition to the burgeoning food scene and the perceptive menu design is fitting for a postcode that proudly parades its East End roots while embracing the attention it receives from other quarters.

Mon–Thur 11am–12am		
Fri–Sat 12am–1:30am		
Sun 10am–11pm	Hoxton	26, 48, 55, N26, N55
Opening times	**Tube**	**Bus**

The Marksman

Grilled quail and burnt bay bread sauce

SERVES 4

4 quails, butterflied
2 lemons, halved

For the brine:
500 ml (2 cups) water
500 ml (2 cups) beer (preferably
    a good ale)
3 tbsp salt
sprigs of thyme
10 peppercorns
1 chilli, split lengthways
1 lemon, sliced

For the bread sauce:
6 bay leaves on the stem
600 ml (2½ cups) full-fat milk
6 cloves
6 peppercorns
1 onion, sliced
pinch of nutmeg
pinch of salt
6 slices day-old white bread, cut into
    small cubes

In the restaurant this dish is cooked over the barbecue, as it results in the intense smoky flavour we are looking to achieve. When serving, we make a reduction of chicken stock and brown butter and drizzle it over the quails.

For the brine, put the ingredients in a large bowl and add the quails. Leave overnight in the fridge.

For the bread sauce, start by burning the bay leaf stem over a barbecue or gas hob, until the leaves go black. Place in a pan with the milk, cloves, peppercorns, onion, nutmeg and salt. Bring to the boil, turn off the heat and cover the pan. Leave to infuse for about 1 hour. (In the restaurant we do this a day ahead, as the flavour of the infusion becomes more intense.)

Sieve the milk infusion into another pan, add the bread and cook over a medium heat for 15 minutes, or until the sauce thickens to a sauce consistency.

Grill the quails on the barbecue until cooked through (this will take about 10 minutes on each side, depending on the heat of the barbecue). (Alternatively, cook in a preheated oven at 180°C/350°F for 15–20 minutes, until cooked through.) Chop the quails in half.

Grill the lemons, flesh-side down, until charred.

To serve, place the bread sauce on the bottom of serving dishes, pile the quails on top and serve the lemons to the side.

The Clove Club

Shoreditch Town Hall, 380 Old Street EC1V 9LT
+44 (0)20 7729 6496 / www.thecloveclub.com

Shoreditch Town Hall has a long and illustrious history, having been built in 1865 and used as a local government base until the 1960s. After doing its bit for politics, it was earmarked for cultural endeavours and is now also home to one of the most exciting London restaurants of recent years.

When it was opened by head chef Isaac McHale (of Young Turks acclaim), Johnny Smith and Daniel Willis, The Clove Club followed in the success of Isaac's previous pop-up supper club ventures, which pushed forward the frontiers of the capital's dining scene and showcased the talents and creativity of a new generation of professional kitchen superstars.

The food offering is all things British, with a smattering of oft-overlooked ingredients, and features a set five-course or extended menu that changes daily to ensure the best quality ingredients are brought to the table. The daily change allows the team to really test their skills each morning and to react not only to marketplace goodies but also to flashes of inspiration in time for the lunch service.

Now in proud possession of a Michelin star, the restaurant continues to impress the public and critics alike with its gorgeously presented but unpretentious plates and winning combination of laid-back dining with exemplary service. An open kitchen, utilitarian tiles and naked wooden tables put diners at ease while dishes such as Raw Orkney Scallop, Flamed Cornish Mackerel, and Yorkshire Suckling Pig put smiles on their faces.

A fine drinks menu keeps the large bar area bustling and there's no need to order a packet of peanuts here, with Venison Sausages and Ketchup, or the ever-popular Buttermilk Fried Chicken and Pine Salt to help soak up the alcohol.

The Clove Club became the first restaurant in the capital to charge diners for their meal when they book a reservation. Having seen profits in previous places of employ decimated by no-shows, it seemed an obvious move. It's hard to argue with the logic and it's likely that in booking etiquette – as well as food – The Clove Club will be a trailblazer.

Opening times	Train	Bus
Mon 6pm–11:30pm **Tue–Sat** 12pm–4pm, 6pm–11:30pm **Sun** Closed	⇄ Shoreditch High Street	 26, 48, 67, 242, 35

Anchor & Hope

36 The Cut SE1 8LP
+44 (0)20 7928 9898 / www.anchorandhopepub.co.uk

This long established dining room in Waterloo is a true pioneer of the oft-bandied term 'gastro pub'. However, this fails to really do justice to the hearty dishes that utilise seasonal ingredients and the best of British to upscale the pie and a pint pub-dining era to something equally as comforting but far more palate-pleasing.

The link to St. John at this establishment is that it was founded by two former chefs who took the wholesome approach to nose-to-tail eating and cleverly adapted it to an after-work, laid-back customer base looking for a decent bite to eat in a pub environment. There's a cosy feel in the Anchor & Hope – no fancy adornments or decorations, just a simple pairing of rich colours and wooden floors and tables. And as for the food, the sharing plates that the dining room has become known for helped to expand the convivial vibe of Sunday lunch or dinner to any day of the week.

Expect to find more unusual meaty cuts and ingredients on the menu – think lamb neck, rabbit, snails and duck hearts – but there's also fresh pasta, steak (Dexter sirloin), native Middle White pork and enough vegetarian options to offer choice rather than dictation. Proper desserts and cheeses round off the meal, while the extensive wine menu – which is almost exclusively French – offers a good range that means you don't have to blow the budget on the drinks bill.

The Anchor & Hope has become part of its landscape and is as much a locals' watering hole as a destination diner. They don't take reservations but that's not exactly a hardship once you've perused the drinks list and perched yourself in the bar area to wait for a table. The time will pass quickly and the parade of orders heading to tables through the dividing curtain will only serve to whet your appetite further.

Opening times	Tube	Bus
Mon 5pm–11pm **Tue–Sat** 11am–11pm **Sun** 12:30pm–3:15pm	Southwark	45, 63, 100, N63, N89

DOWN THE MARKETS

London food markets are as old as the city itself, with some still operating on the same sites as they have done for hundreds of years.

Naturally, the spaces and stock have evolved and hugely diversified – specialist and farmers' markets allow Londoners to buy artisan produce with a global provenance right on their doorsteps – but savvy shoppers still haggle over fish at Billingsgate, buy their meat at Smithfields and banter with the barrow boys at Broadway.

Supermarkets might offer convenience but, despite their vastness, the shelves can be limited; markets provide a colourful and hugely rewarding dimension to the food basket, as well as interaction with producers and a shopping experience that engages all the senses.

From rare breed and sustainable meat, seafood direct from the fishing boats of Cornwall, to locally sourced or exotic seasonal fruit and vegetables, urban honey and artisan breads, cheeses and condiments, London's markets are a treasure trove of culinary goodies. They have also helped to bolster the burgeoning food revolution that has seen the city elevated to centre stage on the world's culinary scene. It would be impossible to do justice to all the many markets that are dotted around the capital but here are some highlights.

BOROUGH

8 Southwark Street SE1 1TL
+44 (0)20 7407 1002 / www.boroughmarket.org.uk

Without a doubt, Borough is the icing on the cake of London's food market scene. If you pause and glance up from the stalls when you're passing through, you'll notice a blue plaque – installed in 2012 – which acknowledges Borough as London's oldest fruit and vegetable market.

The provenance and clientele have certainly changed over the centuries, with livestock making way for lattes and the fruity language of the area's fishwives being replaced by the animated chatter of tourists and artisan traders. However, this corner of the capital has been purveying its foodstuffs since the 11th century and the current location has been in continual use as a food market since the 13th century.

Borough has been written about and photographed as often and widely as any of the great London attractions and that's simply because it has become one of them. Previously the domain of food-conscious locals, restaurateurs and culinary tourists, the market is now a must-visit location that offers a vast range of freshly prepared global hot foods and over one hundred stalls trading in high-end groceries and gourmet treats.

The queue for Monmouth Coffee on Saturday morning is the stuff of local legend but it's all part of the experience and the wait simply serves to build up an appetite for the wares of one of the myriad stalls, cafes, bars and restaurants that fill the air with heady aromas. You can travel the world in one lunchtime with popular takeout options including vegetarian food from Ethiopian Flavours, Indian street food from Gujarati Rasoi, spicy sausages from The German Deli, hot meat baguettes from Hobbs Meat Roast, or a salt beef beigel from Nana Fanny's – to name just a few from the long list of traders.

If you prefer to linger over lunch, you could browse the menus of Fish!, Brindisa or Roast, and perhaps wander back into the fray for a heart-clogging chocolate brownie or Portuguese tart, or take the virtuous route and stock up on your five a day from Borough stalwart, Turnips.

Mon–Thur 10am–5pm Fri 10am–6pm Sat 8am–5pm	London Bridge	43, 141, 149, 521
Market days	**Train and Tube**	**Bus**

Gourmet Goat

Kid goat moussaka

SERVES 4

1 aubergine (eggplant) (about
    350 g/12 oz)

1 tbsp salt

50 ml (3 tbsp) olive oil

1 red onion, diced

1 clove garlic, crushed

500 g (18 oz) high-welfare minced
    (ground) kid goat

1 tbsp baharat

1 tbsp tomato paste

100 ml (½ cup) vegetable stock

350 g (12 oz) potatoes, peeled and
    thinly sliced

salt and freshly ground
    black pepper, to season

Baharat is a Middle Eastern spice blend that is used to season meat and flavour soups and stews. You can find it in ethnic supermarkets, delis and an increasing number of supermarkets.

Chop the aubergine (eggplant) into 2-cm (¾-in) cubes and place in a colander. Sprinkle over the salt (to extract any bitterness) and leave for at least 30 minutes.

Heat 1 tablespoon of the olive oil in a large pan and shallow fry the onion and garlic until soft and translucent.

Add the meat and brown for about 5 minutes.

Stir in the baharat followed by the tomato paste and stock. Cook through for 1 minute. Season with salt and pepper and set aside.

Rinse the aubergine (eggplant) with iced water and pat dry. Shallow fry in 1 tablespoon of olive oil until soft and golden. Remove with a slotted spoon and place on kitchen towel.

Preheat the oven to 200°C (400°F).

Place the meat mixture and aubergine (eggplant) in an ovenproof dish. Layer the potatoes on top and brush with the remaining olive oil. Add a pinch of salt. Bake in the oven for 35 minutes or until the potatoes are cooked and golden.

Serve with a leafy salad dressed with lemon juice and olive oil.

BROADWAY

London Fields E8
www.broadwaymarket.co.uk

Located in the heart of Hackney, Broadway market is a local landmark and traders have been selling their wares here since the 1890s. Hackney has undergone massive gentrification in recent years and this, combined with its rich, cultural and ethnic diversity, has resulted in a Saturday food market that rivals anything the capital has to offer. That's not to say that every stall is an artisan baker or local honey producer (although seek and ye shall find); the market still caters to the local community and is staunchly proud of its East End roots.

In fact, it's a great source of local pride that the market is here at all: having witnessed a slow demise in the eighties and nineties, the market was relaunched by the Broadway Market Traders' and Residents' Association in 2004 with around 40 stalls and now hosts over 135 pitches.

Barrow boys and butchers sell fruit and vegetables and prime cuts to local shoppers, while Hackney hipsters snack on global street food or sip coffee in Climpson & Sons. For a real taste of the East End, you can park your shopping bags and pull up a chair at F. Cooke, which has been serving traditional pie and mash and jellied eels for over 100 years.

Broadway Market is a successful melting pot of traditional stalls and modern street market and it proves that there's an appetite for both, as the street fills up soon after its 9am official opening on Saturday mornings. If you're on a serious shopping mission, arrive early; those on a more leisurely schedule of people watching with a caffeine hit can take their time.

Sat 9am–5pm	London Fields	236, 394
Market days	**Train**	**Bus**

The Richmond
Steak tartare

SERVES 4

200 g (8 oz) diced lean beef
2 tbsp finely diced shallot
2 tbsp finely diced chives
2 tbsp finely diced gherkins
1 tbsp roughly chopped green
    peppercorns
4 fresh free-range eggs
shoestring fries, to serve

For the dressing:
1½ tbsp Dijon mustard
1 tbsp sherry vinegar
1 tbsp water
100 ml (½ cup) vegetable oil
few dashes Tabasco
few dashes Worcestershire sauce

The Richmond is just a short stroll away from bustling Broadway Market. Brett Redman is the chef-owner of this neighbourhood bar and restaurant, which serves traditional fare using locally sourced ingredients, including a range of 35-day-aged Black Angus steaks. It also features an oyster bar with a daily oyster happy hour.

In a large bowl, mix together all the ingredients for the tartare, apart from the eggs. Add the dressing ingredients and mix well to combine.

Divide the mixture equally between four serving plates, forming into patty shapes. Carefully crack open the eggs, one at a time, and place one on the top of each portion of tartare.

At The Richmond we serve this with homemade shoestring fries on the side.

BILLINGSGATE

Trafalgar Way E14 5ST
+44 (0)20 7987 1118 / www.billingsgatefishmarket.org

London restaurants and fishmongers flock to this iconic indoor market to stock their counters and, although Billingsgate is essentially a wholesale market, canny seafood fans can also visit to buy direct from suppliers at a fraction of the retail cost. But don't expect to turn up and be able to buy a couple of salmon fillets for dinner – you'll be buying in bulk and will need to clear some serious space in your freezer before you go. You'll also need to set your alarm, as trading begins at 4am and you should arrive well before the 8am closing time in order to bag the best fish.

Billingsgate has been trading on its current site in Docklands since 1982, well before the influx of the international banks and skyscrapers that dot the landscape today. Previously, the market was located on Lower Thames Street and the original building is now home to vast event spaces.

Like New Covent Garden, Smithfield and other wholesale London markets, Billingsgate is populated with traders and porters whose career paths have followed that of many previous generations. The noise is incredible, with dealing and banter traded in equal measure inside the vast Market Hall. Here, some 40 traders sell about 150 different varieties of fish and seafood, while an army of porters ferry boxes of fish to and from the vast cold stores, deftly navigating the narrow pathways that criss-cross the wet floor.

As well as native British species, you'll find varieties from all over the world, driven overnight from ports around the UK, or arriving by freight plane and chilling in vats of ice while buyers haggle over quality and price. Even if you don't have space to accommodate a box of herring or half a dozen live lobsters, it's a fascinating place to visit and although just a stone's throw from London's financial hub, it feels like light years away.

Tue–Sat 4am–8am	Canary Wharf	277
Market days	**Tube**	**Bus**

Swordfish kebabs with dipping sauce

SERVES 6

900 g (2 lb) swordfish, cut into bite-sized
    cubes
bunch fresh flat-leaf parsley, roughly
    chopped
bunch fresh coriander (cilantro), roughly
    chopped

For the dipping sauce:

125 ml (½ cup) sake
125 ml (½ cup) mirin
3 tbsp soy sauce

Billingsgate sells a huge variety of native British and exotic fish and seafood. Swordfish is a firm, meaty fish that lends itself to short, intense cooking and strong flavour accompaniments.

Soak 12 wooden skewers in water for at least 30 minutes before using.

Add the ingredients for the dipping sauce to a small pan and bring to the boil. Reduce the heat and simmer for about 15 minutes, until the liquid has reduced.

Thread the swordfish onto bamboo skewers, ensuring there are the same number of cubes on each skewer.

Divide the dipping sauce between two bowls and set one aside for serving. Brush the fish with the marinade from the other bowl. Place the skewers over a prepared charcoal grill or under a conventional grill, and cook for 2 minutes on each side, brushing often with the remaining sauce.

Transfer the skewers to a serving dish and garnish with the herbs. Serve with the reserved sauce for dipping.

Salmon en papillote

SERVES 4

4 x 150 g (5 oz) salmon fillets
2 red bell peppers, thickly sliced
1 onion, thickly sliced
2 tbsp olive oil
juice of 1 lemon
salt and freshly ground black pepper,
    to season

A simple way to enjoy a piece of good-quality fresh fish – any firm fish fillet can be cooked using this method.

Preheat the oven to 180°C (350°F).

Cut out four large pieces of baking parchment (these need to be a lot bigger than the fish fillets). Divide the sliced peppers and onions between the baking parchment, arrange in the centre and drizzle over a little olive oil.

Place a salmon fillet on top of each pile of vegetables and squeeze over the lemon juice. Season with salt and pepper.

Pull up two edges of the baking parchment and fold over at the top. Fold in the sides to create a parcel, ensuring there is space around the fish so the steam can move around inside the parcels.

Bake in the oven for 18–20 minutes, until the fish is cooked through. Serve the fish in the paper so the aromas are released when you open the parcels.

MALTBY STREET

Ropewalk SE1 3PA
www.maltby.st

The London food scene is constantly evolving and Maltby Street Market is a fairly recent addition to the artisan market landscape. What began in 2010 as an experiment by a few trailblazing traders who couldn't (or didn't want to) cough up the hefty pitch fees down the road in Borough Market, has become an unprecedented success.

Tucked away under and alongside the railway arches on Ropewalk, in a less salubrious quarter of the capital, the fledgling collection of stallholders joined the existing wholesale distributors and warehouses that were already operating in the area. As the public embraced this new – less frenetic – food enclave, more outlets moved in and the wholesalers opened up their doors and kitchens to the appreciative visitors. It's now a weekend staple for locals and in-the-know foodies. In fact, rock up around lunchtime on a Saturday and you'll be dodging the crowds to bag a seat at a food stall or inside one of many quirky little pop-up bars and restaurants.

If gin is your tipple of choice, you can quench your thirst at Little Bird Gin, or sample locally distilled drinks at Jensen's Gin, enjoy outstanding cured ham at Tozino – London's first jamon bodega; or tuck into Dorset oysters and a glass of champagne while you watch the crowds amble past at Market Gourmet.

Aside from the hungry lunchtime crowd, people also travel to the area to seek out quality ingredients, with traders such as O'Shea's Butchers supplying the public and restaurants.

A five-minute walk away, Spa Terminus is home to another group of food and drink traders. Although not technically part of Maltby Street Market, the two are intrinsically linked: while Maltby Street has become a street food emporium, Spa Terminus is primarily for wholesale businesses, apart from Saturday mornings when many of them open their doors to the public. A number of the original Maltby Street residents have now relocated here to take advantage of longer leases and to concentrate on other areas of their business.

Sat 9am–4pm **Sun** 11am–4pm	Bermondsey	C10, 47, 381, N199
Market days	**Tube**	**Bus**

Sherry-marinated octopus

SERVES 4–6

900 g (2 lb) baby octopus, cleaned

8 fresh plum tomatoes, cut in half

225 g (1 1/3 cups) pitted Kalamata olives,
  halved

100 g (2/3 cup) pimento-stuffed green olives,
  drained and diced

25 g (1 cup) finely chopped parsley,
  to garnish

For the sherry marinade:

50 ml (1/4 cup) olive oil

6 garlic cloves, minced

50 ml (1/4 cup) dry sherry

1 tsp paprika

1/2 tsp fine sea salt

Maltby Street is home to a number of pop-up cafes and restaurants that celebrate international flavours. Octopus is quick and easy to cook and is a popular snack in tapas bars in the area.

For the marinade, combine all the ingredients in a bowl. Pour half the marinade into a sealable plastic bag and set aside the bowl with the remaining marinade to serve.

Place the octopus in the bag, seal and marinate in the refrigerator for up to 12 hours.

Preheat the oven to 230°C (450°F).

Arrange the tomatoes in a roasting pan and drizzle with a little of the reserved marinade. Roast the tomatoes for 10 minutes or until beginning to soften and brown. Remove the octopus from the marinade – do not pat dry – and add to the tomatoes in the roasting pan. Return the pan to the oven and roast for 3–5 minutes or until the octopus is white and opaque.

Combine the octopus and tomatoes with the remaining reserved marinade and the olives. Transfer to a large serving platter, or divide between serving plates, and garnish with parsley.

BRIXTON

Electric Avenue SW9 8JX
www.brixtonmarket.net

Although there is a daily, permanent market on Station Road and Electric Avenue in Brixton, the market scene also encompasses a number of other, smaller markets in the immediate vicinity over different days of the week. This very much reflects the changing nature of the area, which continues to attract hip young things looking for a culturally rich area to live, work or hang out.

The main market is exactly what you'd expect from a traditional high street market, bar the fact that it is owned and run by the traders – the Brixton Market Traders' Federation Community Interest Company to be precise. This means it's very community oriented and it's a bustling, noisy and friendly place to buy all manner of everyday and exotic ingredients, as well as clothes, housewares and general bric-a-brac.

Once you've explored the outdoor market, you can step into one of the arcades – Brixton Village and Market Row – to continue shopping. Here you'll find an incredible selection of world foods, from dried fish to dried herbs, along with pop-up shops and quirky boutiques. However, in recent years, it's the influx of cafes, restaurants and bars that has really put Brixton Village, in particular, on the foodie map. Forward-thinking small chains such as Champagne + Fromage, Honest Burgers, and Federation, and independents like French & Grace, and Senzala Creperie went out on a limb to create a food-lovers' emporium in this arcade and to say they've made a success of it is an understatement.

But the culinary adventure doesn't end there: you can wind down for the weekend at Friday Market, which combines street food with crafts, while Sundays see Brixton Station Road lined with stalls selling preserves, free-range meat, dairy produce and fresh fruit and vegetables at the weekly farmers' market. And, if the combination of tucking into a cake while rummaging through a rail of secondhand clothes floats your boat, then check out the Bakers' & Flea market on the first Saturday of the month.

Daily	Brixton	P5, 322, 35
Market days	**Tube**	**Bus**

Jamaican patties

MAKES 10–12

400 g (3¼ cups) plain (all-purpose) flour
1 tsp salt, plus extra to season
50 ml (¼ cup) cooking oil
½ tsp ground cumin
1 small onion, finely chopped
½ tsp red chilli powder
¼ tsp turmeric
3 medium potatoes, boiled and finely diced
75 g (½ cup) frozen peas, thawed
2 tbsp chopped coriander (cilantro)
beaten egg, to glaze

Brixton has a strong Afro-Caribbean heritage and this is evident in the stalls and cafes in and around the market. These subtly spiced patties are typical market fare.

Mix the flour with the salt and 2 tablespoons of the oil. Knead with sufficient water to form a smooth, soft dough. Divide the dough into golf-ball-sized balls, cover with a damp towel and set aside for 15–20 minutes.

Heat the remaining oil in a large wok and add the ground cumin. Add the onion and fry until it softens.

Stir in chilli powder, turmeric and season with salt. Sauté for a few seconds, then add the potatoes and peas and mix well to combine. Cook for a few minutes to allow the flavours to blend, stirring occasionally. Stir in the chopped coriander (cilantro). Set aside to cool to room temperature.

Preheat the oven to 200°C (400°F).

Lightly flour the work surface and roll out the dough to form flat circles about 5-mm (¼-inch) thick. Place a heaped spoon of the filling onto each circle, leaving a border. Brush the beaten egg around the edge then fold over the patties, sealing well around the edges.

Place the patties spaced apart on 1 or 2 large, greased baking trays. Bake in the oven for 20–25 minutes, until golden brown and cooked through.

BRICK LANE

The Old Truman Brewery, 152 Brick Lane E1 6RU
www.boilerhouse-foodhall.co.uk

Brick Lane isn't just one market, more a collection of different markets that ebb and flow through the area on different days, offering a vast selection of food and drink from the UK and all over the world.

The Boiler House Food Hall, located at the Old Truman Brewery, is where you'll be spoilt for choice on your weekend London food tour. You can choose from top quality, freshly cooked global snacks and plates. Unlike some other markets, where you jostle for a bit of space to stand and micromanage cutlery, cartons and personal belongings, The Boiler House has tables and bench seating to enjoy a more leisurely lunch.

If you like to combine food with a bit of retail therapy, Sunday Upmarket offers the best of both worlds, with over 140 stalls that showcase the talents of new designers alongside the cooking skills of indie food producers and chefs. The street food hall is almost overwhelming in its variety and the quality of cuisine on offer with hot food from pretty much every country or region you can name.

Japanese sushi, pad Thai, Tibetan dumplings and piquant satay vie for your attention on behalf of Asia, while the Pan-American selection includes Caribbean curries, Brazilian hot dogs and Venezuelan cachapa. There's also plenty of representation from across Europe and the Middle East, with cakes, sweets and pastries filling the gap for those with a sweet tooth.

There's usually a loud soundtrack playing in the hall to accompany the many circuits around the stalls that you'll need to complete before deciding what to eat. Whatever you choose, it will be the right decision.

Sat 11am–6pm
Sun 10am–5pm

Market days

Shoreditch High Street

Train

67, 8, 388, N8

Bus

Yakisoba

For the sauce:

3 tbsp teriyaki sauce

2 tbsp mirin (rice wine) or apple juice

2 tsp hot chilli sauce

1 lemongrass stalk, inner core only, crushed and finely sliced

1 tsp sugar

2 tsp sesame oil

For the stir-fry:

225 g (8 oz) soba noodles

1½ tbsp sunflower oil

1 small onion, sliced

2 garlic cloves, minced

2 carrots, thinly sliced

½ head cabbage, shredded

225 g (8 oz) firm tofu, pressed, drained, and cut into 1-cm (½-in) cubes

4 spring onions (scallions), chopped, plus extra to garnish

1 tbsp toasted sesame seeds

pickled ginger, to garnish (optional)

This is a classic Japanese street-food dish of the type sold at stalls in Brick Lane. Combine the sauce ingredients in a small bowl and set aside.

Cook the soba noodles in boiling water for about 2 minutes or until they are just cooked. Do not overcook or the noodles become sticky. Drain, rinse in cold water then drain again.

Heat the oil in a large skillet or wok over a medium-high heat. Add the onion and stir-fry for 2 minutes, then add the garlic, carrots and cabbage. Stir-fry for 3–5 minutes, until the vegetables are cooked but still firm.

Add the tofu, soba noodles, spring onions (scallions), sesame seeds and sauce, then cook, tossing to combine, until the noodles and tofu are hot. Serve garnished with chopped spring onions (scallions) or seaweed and strips of pickled ginger, if liked.

Mushroom fajitas

SERVES 4

750 g (1½ lb) Portobello mushrooms
1 large onion, sliced into thick rounds
1 red bell pepper, cut into quarters
vegetable oil, for brushing
salt and freshly ground black pepper, to
    season
flour tortillas, guacamole and
    pico de gallo, to serve

For the pico de gallo:
1 medium onion, finely chopped
4 tomatoes, deseeded and finely diced
1 jalapeño pepper, finely chopped
bunch of coriander (cilantro), chopped
1 clove garlic, crushed
juice of 1 lime
salt and freshly ground black pepper,
    to season

Another classic market snack, these fajitas are served with a generous helping of pico de gallo – a fresh Mexican salad made from chopped onion, tomato, jalepeños and coriander (cilantro). The ingredients are all finely chopped so it's more like a salsa.

Prepare a hot barbecue or heat a cast-iron fajita pan on the hob until very hot.

Brush the mushrooms, onion slices and bell pepper with vegetable oil and season with salt and pepper.

Grill the onion and pepper for 5–7 minutes per side, or until charred and softened.

Grill the mushrooms for 1½–2 minutes per side, or until they have good grill marks.

For the pico de gallo, combine all the ingredients in a bowl and season with salt and pepper.

Slice the mushrooms on the diagonal and serve with the grilled vegetables, tortillas, guacamole and pico de gallo.

STREET FEAST

You only have to look at the likes of Pitt Cue Co. (page 84) and BAO (page 86) to appreciate London's appetite for incredible street food. These successful restaurants began life as pop-ups and food vans but such was their popularity that they were able to upscale to permanent premises and expand their repertoire and clientele base.

The food revolution continues to take the capital by storm and Street Feast has taken the phenomenon to another level by setting up evening food markets in various locations around London. There's something of a festival vibe at these weekly events, with DJs and cocktail bars complementing the vast array of quality food stalls and pop-ups that are dotted around the venues. They're all open until late, which means after-work drinkers and families can head over early, before making way for more serious partygoers after dark when the music is cranked up.

The brainchild of events organiser Dominic Cools-Lartigue, and Milk & Honey founder Jonathan Downey, Street Feast has taken over oft-forgotten spaces and actually rejuvenated some of the areas the markets inhabit. Lewisham Model Market is a case in point, as the old dilapidated indoor market has been given a hip new lease of life and brought a huge amount of commerce to the area – this has had a knock-on effect towards the overall gentrification of SE13, which is now experiencing something of an underground food revolution.

Dinerama and Hawker House open all year; Model Market **April to September**

www.streetfeast.com

Hawker House, Canada Water
Fri and Sat 5pm to late

Dinerama, Shoreditch
Thurs, Fri, Sat 5pm to late

Model Market, Lewisham
Fri, Sat 5pm to late

Mama's Jerk
Jerk barbecue chicken

SERVES 4–6

1 x 2 kg (4½ lb) free-range chicken, split in
half butterfly style

For the jerk marinade:
2 Scotch Bonnet chillies, sliced
½ bunch fresh thyme, chopped
4 garlic cloves, chopped
1 bunch spring onions (scallions), chopped
2 tbsp ground allspice
2 tbsp salt
2 tsp ground black pepper
2 tbsp natural honey
juice of 1 lime
2 tbsp pineapple juice
125 ml (½ cup) oil
125 ml (½ cup) water

Mama's Jerk is a regular at a number of Street Feast locations.

Blend the marinade ingredients, using a hand blender, until it forms a thick paste.
Lightly score the chicken with a sharp knife.

Rub the meat with the marinade (set aside some for basting) then refrigerate for
24 hours so it is infused with the marinade.

Grill the chicken slowly over a preheated grill (preferably a charcoal and wood-
smoke barbecue), turning and basting every 15–20 minutes with the remaining
marinade. It will take about 30–45 minutes for the chicken to be fully cooked with a
crisp, golden skin.

Cover with foil and cool by moving and spreading out the charcoal and wood to one
side in the barbecue.

Serve with roasted jerk-spiced sweet potatoes, corn on the cob, grilled or fried
plantain, coleslaw or classic rice and peas.

Club Mexicana
Barbecue pulled jackfruit

SERVES 8–10

60 ml (¼ cup) vegetable oil
2 Jalapeños, finely chopped
6 cloves garlic, finely chopped
1 tbsp chilli powder
2 tsp cumin
½ tsp cayenne
500 ml (2 cups) ketchup
125 ml (½ cup) lime juice
200 g (1 cup) dark brown sugar
4 cans jackfruit in brine
1 tbsp Dijon mustard

To serve:
corn tacos, shredded cos lettuce,
guacamole, fresh lime juice, chopped
coriander (cilantro)

Club Mexicana prepares vegan street food at markets around London.

Heat 2 tablespoons of the oil in a pan and fry the jalapeños and garlic for
1 minute. Add the chilli powder, cumin and cayenne and cook, stirring constantly,
until fragrant (1–2 minutes).

Add the ketchup, lime juice and sugar and stir until the sugar is dissolved. Partially
cover and cook over a low heat until the sauce has thickened to the consistency
of ketchup.

Drain and rinse the jackfruit. Tear the strands of jackfruit from the harder core: the
fruit will come apart easily. Put the fruit in a bowl.

Heat the remaining oil in a pan and add the jackfruit strands. Cook until it becomes
grey and loses some moisture. Add the mustard and stir.

Add half the barbecue sauce and stir well to combine. The jackfruit should be just
coated in barbecue sauce – add more, as needed. Cook until it's starting to get a little
crispy and sticking to the pan. Spoon on top of warm tacos and top with lettuce,
guacamole, a squeeze of fresh lime juice and a sprinkle of chopped coriander
(cilantro).

LONDON FARMERS' MARKETS

lfm.org.uk

Although there are many farmers' markets in the capital, those that are run by the London Farmers' Markets organisation have specific requirements of their sellers, to ensure consistency of quality for consumers, as well as a fair price for traders.

In order to take a stall at one of the markets, the producers have to raise, grow or bake everything they sell on their stall. The markets are all certified by the Farmers' Retail and Markets Association (FARMA). As well as running the markets, the organisation also offers advice to producers and actively supports sustainable farming and traditional breeds and ensures the highest quality produce and products are available locally to Londoners.

The markets operate in all corners of the capital and there are a number during the week so you can get your fill of fruit and veg outside the usual weekend slots. Here's the full list of the 23 markets that are run by the team.

The markets

Balham
Saturday 9am–1pm
Henry Cavendish Primary School
Hydethorpe Road
SW12 0JA

Blackheath
Sunday 10am–2pm
Blackheath Station Car Park
SE3 9LA

Bloomsbury
Thursday 9am–2pm
Torrington Square, Byng Place
WC1E 7HY

Dulwich Village
Saturday 10am–2pm
Dulwich Church of England Infant
School, Turney Road
SE21 7BN

Ealing
Saturday 9am–1pm
Leeland Road W13 9HH

Earls Court
Sunday 10am–2pm
St. Cuthbert with St. Matthias School,
Warwick Road
SW5 9UE

Highgate Hill
Sunday 10am–2pm
St. Joseph's Junior School
N19 5NE

Islington
Sunday 10am–2pm
Chapel Market N1 9PZ

London Bridge
Tuesday 9am–2pm
King's College London
Guys Campus
SE1 1UL

Marylebone
Sunday 10am–2pm
Cramer Street Car Park
W1U 4EW

Notting Hill
Saturday 9am–1pm
Kensington Church Street
W11 3LQ

Parliament Hill
Saturday 10am–2pm
William Ellis School
NW5 1RN

Parson's Green
Sunday 10am–2pm
Thomas's Academy
New King's Road
SW6 4LY

Pimlico Road
Saturday 9am–1pm
Orange Square
SW1W 8UT

Queens Park
Sunday 10am–2pm
Salusbury Primary School, Salusbury
Road NW6 6RG

South Kensington (Bute Street)
Saturday 9am–2pm
Bute Street SW7 3EX

South Kensington
(Queen's Lawn)
Tuesday 9am–2pm
Queen's Lawn SW7 5NH

Swiss Cottage
Wednesday 10am–3pm
Eton Avenue
NW3 3EU

Twickenham
Saturday 9am–1pm
Holly Road Car Park
TW1 4HF

Walthamstow
Sunday 10am–2pm
Town Square, off High Street
E17 7JN

West Hampstead
Saturday 10am–2pm
West Hampstead Thameslink Station
forecourt, Iverson Road NW6 1PF

West Hill
Sunday 10am–2pm
West Hill Primary School
Merton Road
SW18 5ST

Wimbledon
Saturday 9am–1pm
Wimbledon Park Primary School
Havana Road
SW19 8EJ

IN THE NEIGHBOURHOOD

London has always been a culinary and culturally diverse city: as the centre of the country's trading routes from the 16th century (when the East India Company was established), the city embraced the exotic ingredients that arrived at its docks and became home to a global population that introduced new foods, cooking styles and cuisines to the capital.

Today, the legacy of trade, migration and culinary curiosity very much lives on and certain areas of London that were historically settled by adventurers and traders have become synonymous with their cultures. The original flavours of 'home' have evolved into a proud heritage of national, regional and fusion food, and areas with strong cultural and social links to other countries.

These areas have become go-to destinations for authentic global food, offering a wonderful array of everything from modest, family run cafes to world renowned restaurants that cater to locals and food travellers alike.

CHINATOWN

Chinatown was only established in its current location in the West End following the war, when returning service personnel went searching for restaurants that served the cuisine they'd enjoyed in the Far East. Prior to this, a small Chinese community had established itself alongside the docks in Limehouse – largely consisting of sailors and their families. The draw of central London was the cosmopolitan restaurant scene and, as the pioneers of the new Chinatown became successful with their business ventures, so more followed.

Chinatown centres around Gerrard Street, just off Shaftesbury Avenue, and it's a vibrant area filled with Chinese restaurants, cafes, shops and herbal medicine practitioners. It's colourful, noisy and compact, with the aromas of a hundred hot kitchens pumping out into the streets and ensuring you don't walk through without stopping for a bite to eat. With so much choice it's hard to know which restaurant door to enter but you'll be in safe hands if you step over the threshold of the likes of Young Cheng for incredible dim sum; Imperial China for authentic Cantonese food; and Yauatcha if you want to discover what Michelin Chinese food tastes like. If you don't have time for a lengthy repast, at the very least you need to try some steamed buns – pop into Kowloon for takeout cakes, buns and dumplings.

Finally, if you're inspired to recreate any dishes for yourself at home, supermarkets New Moon Lane and See Woo will have all the ingredients you need.

Chinatown is a worthy food destination any time and many of the restaurants and cafes stay open long into the night so it's still busy when the rest of town starts to wind down. But Chinese New Year sees the area awash with music, decorations and dancing and the parade is a popular date in the London calendar.

Leicester Square

Tube

14, 19, 38, N19, N38

Bus

Chinese salt & pepper squid

SERVES 4

450 g (1 lb) baby or medium squid
2 tbsp coarse salt
1 tbsp freshly ground black pepper
2 tbsp rice flour or cornflour (cornstarch)
vegetable or sesame oil, for frying
2 limes, halved

This simple snack is served in restaurants across Chinatown. Cook the squid quickly so the batter is crispy but the squid remains tender.

Prepare the squid by pulling the head apart from the body. Sever the tentacles and trim. Pull out the backbone from inside the body sac and then clean the body inside and out, removing any skin.

Slice the squid into rings, then pat dry and place on a dish with the tentacles. Mix the salt and pepper with the flour, tip it over the squid and toss well to coat evenly.

Heat enough oil in a wok or heavy-based saucepan for deep-frying. Cook the squid rings in batches, until they crisp and turn golden, about 1–2 minutes.

Drain on kitchen towel and serve with lime to squeeze over.

Five-spice chicken with bok choy

SERVES 4

1 tsp five-spice powder
1 tbsp light soy sauce
1 tbsp brown sugar
pinch of pepper
1 tsp crushed red pepper flakes
125 ml (½ cup) water
4 boneless, skinless chicken thighs
1 tbsp rapeseed (canola) oil
3 shallots, sliced
2 garlic cloves, crushed
2 bok choy, stalks sliced horizontally
1 red bell pepper, sliced
sliced spring onions (scallions), to garnish
sliced red chilli, to garnish

It's not easy to replicate the flavours of a Chinese banquet in a domestic kitchen but this quick recipe offers the essence of Chinatown with classic seasonings and still-crunchy peppers and bok choy.

In a large bowl, combine the first six ingredients and set aside.

Slice the chicken crosswise into strips. Heat the oil in a large frying pan and then cook the chicken in batches, over a medium-high heat, until browned. Remove from the pan and keep warm. Repeat, adding a little more oil, if required, until all the chicken is cooked.

Add a little more oil to the pan, if necessary, and stir-fry the shallots for 2 minutes.

Add the garlic and cook for 1 minute. Add the seasoning mixture and bring to the boil. Add the chicken and simmer for 15 minutes, until cooked through.

Add the bok choy stalks and simmer for about 3 minutes to soften. Add the bok choy leaves and pepper and cook for 2 more minutes to heat through.

Serve garnished with sliced spring onions (scallions) and chilli.

SOUTHBANK AND BOROUGH

It doesn't get much better than strolling alongside the Thames, taking in the sights and stopping off for a bite to eat or snacking from a food stall. Southbank has always been a destination for the capital's equivalent of a bracing pre-roast or post-pub country hike but it's also quietly been building a reputation as a hotspot for food lovers.

The obvious culinary draw is Borough Market (page 120), which quite literally has something for everyone and is also home to a number of restaurants of note (Roast and Brindisa are good starting points). While you're there you should also pop into Monmouth Coffee for one of the best caffeine hits in the capital and, of course, a trip this side of town wouldn't be complete without following your nose to Neal's Yard Dairy.

However, SE1 isn't all about Borough Market: walk a little further and delve a little deeper and you'll discover more edible treats. The Southbank Centre Market has been growing in size and reputation over the last couple of years and you'll find a wide variety of artisan ingredients, street food, craft ales and premium coffee from local roasters.

If you'd rather sit down for a more leisurely dining experience, you can take in the incredible river views in Skylon on the third floor of the Festival Hall, or walk a little further along the riverbank to the iconic OXO Tower Restaurant. If a river view isn't a prerequisite for lunch on Southbank, take a turn inland from the river path, where you can enjoy the delights of the newly refurbished Brasserie Blanc.

A little off the beaten track but still easy to find and worth seeking out is the glorious Konditor & Cook. The little bakery is bursting at the seams with freshly baked bread and pastries and a range of hot and cold buffet meals and salads have the locals streaming through the doors at lunchtime.

Waterloo

Train and Tube

1, 4, 26, 59, N343, RV1

Bus

Pecan brownies

MAKES 12

150 g (1¼ sticks) unsalted butter
225 g (8 oz) dark chocolate
2 eggs
150 g (¾ cup) caster (superfine) sugar
few drops vanilla essence
50 g (½ cup) self-raising flour, sifted
100 g (1 cup) pecans, chopped
100 g (4 oz) white chocolate,
   roughly chopped
50 ml (¹/₅ cup) sour cream

The market at Southbank is the perfect place to stop for coffee and snacks during a walk along the river. Chocolate brownies are always on the menu and these are easy to make at home.

Preheat the oven to 190°C (375°F). Grease a 20-cm (8-inch) square cake tin.

Melt the butter and half the dark chocolate in a bowl over a pan of simmering water, then remove from the heat.

In a bowl, beat the eggs, sugar and vanilla until combined. Stir in the melted chocolate mixture. Add the flour, pecans and white chocolate and stir to combine.

Pour into the prepared tin and bake for 30 minutes until the centre is just firm. Place the tin on a wire rack to cool.

Melt the remaining dark chocolate in a bowl over a pan of simmering water. Remove from the heat and stir in the sour cream until smooth.

Spread the frosting over the top of the brownie and chill in the fridge until just set. Cut the brownie into 12 squares. They can be stored in an airtight container in the fridge for up to 4 days.

HARLESDEN

Harlesden has a rich cultural heritage and the area has historically attracted people from all over the world, often for economic reasons. Most notably, a wave of immigration from Ireland, the West Indies and India during the 1960s saw the ethnic mix of the area diversify even further. Today, Harlesden is home to many people with African and Caribbean heritage, as well as growing Portuguese and Brazilian communities.

The many different cultures have had a huge impact on the food and cultural scene in this part of northwest London, with African, Caribbean and Iberian influences, in particular, resulting in an incredible variety of national and regional restaurants that serve the local population, as well as visitors from all over town and beyond.

There are established, family-run eateries like the popular Reggie's, which serves traditional Trinidadian fare (curried goat, fried fish, rice and peas, and fried plantain are all on the menu). If you're in a hurry, the One Stop Caribbean offers great food at reasonable prices – try Callaloo and Saltfish, or Curry Mutton Roti. Duck round the corner and you could be tucking into tapas at the much-feted Centro Galego de Londres or sampling Portuguese specialities at O Bombeiro or Benfica.

Food is very much at the heart of Harlesden. Gentrification has seen the area change a lot over recent years but independent eateries have ensured the character of NW10 has endured – let's hope it stays that way.

⇌	🚌
Harlesden	187, 224, 226, 260, 487
Train	**Bus**

Portuguese roast sardines with coriander & bay

**SERVES 6 as a starter
or snack**

75 g (¹/₃ cup) unsalted butter, softened
20 bay leaves, snipped with scissors
2 tbsp whole coriander seeds
2 tbsp coarse sea salt
about 30 large sardines, cleaned,
   with head and tail intact
1 lemon, thinly sliced
225 ml (1 cup) tarragon vinegar
6 whole black peppercorns
fine sea salt, to season

With its thriving Portuguese community, Harlesden has become a destination in London for Iberian food and culture. Sardines are nothing short of a Portuguese staple and are delicious simply roasted with butter and spices.

Spread 2 tablespoons of the butter over the base of a large roasting pan.

In a bowl, combine the remaining butter with the bay leaves, coriander seeds and salt. Spread the insides of the fish with half of the flavoured butter, then stuff with lemon slices. Place the fish diagonally in the roasting pan, turning the tail up and over, if necessary, to fit. Dot the fish with the remaining flavoured butter. Place in a cold oven and turn the temperature to 230°C (450°F). Roast for 20 minutes, until the fish begins to flake when tested with a fork in the thickest part.

Transfer the fish to a serving platter and cover loosely with foil. Pour the juices from the roasting pan into a large saucepan over a high heat. Stir in the vinegar and peppercorns. Season with sea salt and bring to the boil for 1 minute. Pour the hot sauce over the fish and serve.

SHOREDITCH AND HOXTON

This area of east London has become a dining, drinking and cultural hub for the hip generation over the last 20 years. Previously a neglected area in terms of noteworthy restaurants, the influx of artists, designers and other creative types has fast forwarded gentrification and had restaurateurs, baristas and mixologists clamouring for leases on revamped warehouses, converted factories and new-build developments. The area is awash with galleries and Jay Jopling's White Cube, which opened in 2000, can take at least some of the credit for transforming the area from gritty East End locale into edgy creative enclave.

When it comes to eating out, there's been an explosion of exciting new openings in the area over the years and they keep on coming. There doesn't seem to be a saturation point for quality dining options in this part of town: star turns like Jamie Oliver's Fifteen rub shoulders with the likes of British stalwart Rivington Grill and innovative dining rooms Lyle's (page 102) and The Clove Club, which has taken up residency at Shoreditch Town Hall to great acclaim (page 114).

Of course, it's not all about fine dining – Shoreditch is also a hub of pop-ups, food stalls, global cafes and laid-back fast food. Street food markets are becoming increasingly popular all over London and Shoreditch has a couple of options. Urban Food Fest is a food and drink market that runs every Saturday from midday until midnight in Euro Car Parks on Shoreditch High Street. It regularly features 15 food trucks selling gourmet street food, as well as a bar and cocktail bar. Take a short stroll along the road to Great Eastern Street and you'll find another foodie gem: Dinerama. This is one of four night food markets run by Street Feast (page 148) and the extensive covered site features 15 pop-up restaurants and five bars, as well as music for late-night diners. It's open every Thursday to Sunday from midday until late.

Other options for eating on the hoof include Brick Lane Upmarket (page 140) where you'll be spoilt for choice with a huge array of global fare, while Brick Lane itself is the obvious port of call for trying Indian cuisine. If you're in the area, you should also make a beeline for Old Spitalfields Market where food, boutique clothes and art gather under one roof in the renovated market hall. The market is also home to a number of notable restaurants, including Taberna do Mercado (page 66) while fans of St. John (page 92) need only step across the road to sample Fergus Henderson's carnivore-friendly fare.

Shoreditch High Street   8, 388, N8, 67, 26, 48, 149, N26, N55, 242

Train   **Bus**

Seafood dumplings

SERVES 8

450 g (1 lb) medium raw prawns (shrimp),
  peeled and deveined
2 spring onions (scallions), coarsely chopped
1 tbsp roughly chopped fresh coriander
  (cilantro)
1 tbsp roughly chopped fresh mint
2 tsp soy sauce, plus extra for dipping
2 tbsp double (heavy) cream
48 (9-cm/3½-in diameter) round dumpling
  wrappers
1 large egg, beaten with 2 tbsp water
sea salt, to season

This recipe is inspired by the street markets that are so popular around Shoreditch and which embrace cuisines from all over the world. Dumplings are the ideal party snack so don't be put off by the amount you make, they'll soon disappear.

In a food processor, combine the prawns (shrimp), spring onions (scallions), coriander (cilantro), mint and soy sauce together until finely chopped. Season with sea salt.

Transfer the mixture to a bowl and stir in the cream. Arrange the wrappers on a flat surface. Brush the egg mixture around the perimeter of each wrapper. Place a rounded teaspoon of filling in the centre, then fold the wrapper into a half-moon shape and press the edges together to seal.

Bring a large saucepan of water to the boil. Add the dumplings in batches, and cook until the skins turn transparent and the prawns (shrimp) are pink, about 2 minutes. Drain in a colander and serve warm with soy sauce for dipping.

NEW MALDEN

Affectionately nicknamed 'Little Korea', New Malden in southwest London is – perhaps surprisingly – home to the biggest Korean expat community in Europe. Although most of the 30,000 are from South Korea, many hundreds of North Koreans have fled here over the years to escape troubles in their home country. No one is entirely sure how this unassuming part of town became a magnet for Korean expats but with the South Korean embassy previously located in the area it would have been a natural focal point for new arrivals to London.

With such a large percentage of the New Malden population originating from one other country, it's no wonder that this is the place to come to sample some of the best Korean food in the capital. From street food to barbecue, bulgogi (the popular Korean beef dish) to sushi, it's possible to be totally immersed in Korean food, language and culture just a short hop away from central London.

If you're looking for traditional Korean dishes, then Korea Garden is a good place to start. Small and unassuming from the outside, once you step through the door you're instantly transported to Korea. Another go-to restaurant is Jin Go Gae and this is the place to sample authentic Korean barbecue, as well as bulgogi, soups and pickles.

There's nothing like a spot of karaoke after dinner and, should the mood take you, Han is a comfortable bar with six lounges in which to release your inner diva. It's just opposite the station, so ideal for those travelling in for the evening – and there's a highly rated restaurant upstairs, as well.

When it comes to shopping, Korea Foods is a one-stop shop for Korean – and other Asian – ingredients and groceries. The vast store features a fish counter where a sushi chef will cut fish to order, as well as fresh tofu that is made on site. H Mart is another highly rated local retailer, while Hyun's Bakery will satiate a sweet tooth.

Korean braised beef with gingko nuts

SERVES 4

1 kg (2 lb) beef ribs, cut into 2 or 3 pieces
 and scored with a sharp knife
about 12 gingko nuts, shelled
about 12 shiitake mushrooms, trimmed
 and quartered
2 tbsp toasted sesame seeds

For the marinade:
125 ml (½ cup) soy sauce
125 ml (½ cup) sake
2 tbsp palm sugar
1 tbsp sesame oil
2 tbsp honey
4 garlic cloves, crushed
4 spring onions (scallions), trimmed and
 finely chopped
freshly ground black pepper, to season

Gingko nuts come from the seeds of the gingko biloba tree. They're widely used in Asian cooking and are believed to have a number of health-giving properties due to their high mineral content.

Prepare the marinade. In a large bowl, mix together the soy sauce, sake and sugar until the sugar has dissolved. Beat in the sesame oil and honey, then stir in the garlic and spring onions (scallions). Season with black pepper.

Place the ribs in a shallow dish and pour over the marinade, rubbing it into the ribs. Set aside in the fridge to marinate for at least 2–3 hours.

Transfer the ribs and marinade to a wok or heavy-based pan and pour in roughly 800 ml (3½ cups) of water. Bring the liquid to the boil, then reduce the heat, partially cover the pan and simmer the ribs for 2–3 hours, topping off with more water, if necessary.

Add the gingko nuts and cook for 30 minutes, then add the mushrooms and cook for 15 minutes.

Transfer the ribs to a serving plate and sprinkle with toasted sesame seeds.

Korean roasted sea bass

SERVES 4

4 x (175–225-g/6–8-oz) sea bass fillets,
 rinsed and patted dry
450 g (1 lb) prepared kimchee,
 coarsely chopped

For the kochukaru sauce:
3 tbsp soy sauce
1 tbsp sugar
1 tbsp rice wine
2 tsp sesame oil
2 tbsp kochukaru (Korean chilli
 pepper flakes)
salt and freshly ground black pepper,
 to season

Prepared kimchee is a spicy Korean cabbage relish that is available in larger supermarkets and Korean grocers.

Preheat the oven to 220°C (425°F).

Place the sea bass on an oiled baking tray and lay the kimchee over the top.

Roast for 20–25 minutes or until the fish begins to flake when tested with a fork in the thickest part.

Meanwhile, prepare the sauce. In a saucepan, bring the soy sauce, sugar and rice wine to the boil. Stir to dissolve the sugar. Remove from the heat and stir in the sesame oil and kochukaru. Season with salt and pepper.

Pour the sauce over the fish and serve.

GREENWICH AND BLACKHEATH

Despite the naysayers claiming that everything of worth in London happens north of the river, anyone who lives, works and socialises down south will be happy to list many postcodes where innovative and exciting things are happening in a fast-moving and diverse food scene. Clapham and Battersea are home to some of the best restaurants in town, Brockley has a burgeoning artisan food scene and thriving food market and East Dulwich is home to possibly the most comprehensive culinary high street in London.

However, with space for just one area, Greenwich and Blackheath has made the cut. The newly refurbished Greenwich Market is filled with aromatic smells from all corners of the globe at the weekend, while over in Blackheath, the well supported Farmers' Market takes over the station car park on Sundays. Sticking in Blackheath, the range of independent cafes, delis and restaurants has helped to create a vibrant dining scene. Chapters offers top-notch all-day dining, Buenos Aires bustles like its city namesake as it serves incredible steaks and Bianco 43 outshines pretty much every other Italian eatery within striking distance. Newcomer Le Bouchon (see recipe on the next page) is a classy French wine bar serving snacks and small plates, including a very reasonably priced cheese and charcuterie menu.

Step back over the heath and through Greenwich Park and you can shop at Heap's Sausages – Martin Heap's award-winning sausage emporium. A few roads away and you'll arrive at Guy Awford's gastropub and restaurant, The Guildford, which is a locals' favourite for good reason. The area is also home to a number of craft breweries, including Meantime Brewery in Greenwich and microbrewery Zero Degrees in the heart of Blackheath.

Greenwich or Blackheath

Train

380, 386

Bus

GREENWICH MARKET

sophia & matt

HELTER SKELTER

LIME & POPPY SEED DRIZZLE
A moist lime sponge with poppy seed
topped with a tangy lime drizzle

Vegan

£3.50

LEMON & ROSEMARY
A moist lemon sponge with hints of rosemary
and a sweet, tangy lemon centre

vegan, nut free

£3.50

Le Bouchon
Terrine de canard

MAKES 15 PORTIONS

500 g (17½ oz) pork sausage meat
800 g (1 lb) duck meat
1 onion, chopped
2 bay leaves, chopped
bunch of parsley, chopped
100 ml (½ cup) Armagnac
salt and freshly ground black pepper,
    to season

Le Bouchon is a modern wine bar with an enviable location just off the heath in Blackheath. Wines are served by the glass, carafe or bottle and the simple menu pairs cheese, meats and small plates with the extensive wine list.

This terrine is simple to make and can be served on toast or as an accompaniment to cold plates. The French way to eat it is with grilled bread and cornichons, with a green salad and balsamic vinegar (but any mix of acidity and sweetness will work). At the restaurant, we use duck legs for confit and magrets, so you should use the meat from the throat, wings, belly etc for this dish.

Mince the duck and pork meat finely in a food processor. Add the onion, bay leaves and parsley and mix well to combine.

Add salt and a generous amount of pepper. Slowly add the Armagnac while mixing constantly – all the ingredients should have the same consistency.

Empty the mixture into hermetic jars (we use small 200-g/7-oz jars for better preservation). Cook in a pressure cooker. Wait until it has reached maximum heat and then cook on low heat for 1 hour.

You can keep the jars outside the fridge for 2–3 months, as long as you don't open them. Once open, eat within 24 hours and keep in the fridge.

SOUTHALL

Located in West London, Southall is a vibrant, largely South Asian neighbourhood. Although the early part of the last century saw an influx of Welsh migrants, the largest migration to the area has been from India – and specifically from the Punjab. This migration was most notable just after the Second World War, when London had great need of workers to fuel industrial growth.

Such a large ethnic population from one region has resulted in Southall having some of the best Indian regional food in the capital – if not the country. If you're new to the flavours of the Punjab then Raunka Punjab Diyan will acclimatise you. Themed around a rural Punjabi village, the restaurant is decorated with murals and an extensive menu of classic dishes that will often be enjoyed to a background of live music.

For a change in pace, head down the road to the less frenetic Madhu's. Here, the interior is contemporary and the food fuses Punjabi and Kenyan influences, with dishes like Boozi Bafu (spring lamb chops on the bone) and a fish curry made with Kenyan tilapia helping to win the restaurant a number of awards. When it comes to groceries you're spoilt for choice, with a selection of large Asian supermarkets such as the family-run Dokal and Sons on The Broadway, where it's possible to buy pretty much every Asian and Middle Eastern ingredient you could need.

Head outdoors to Southall Market on Saturday and you'll be transported to India with the huge range of hot food stalls, fruit, veg, incredible herbs and spices, and fresh fish. You'll also find saris, jewellery and homewares.

Southall

Train

95, 105, 195, E5, 120

Bus

Tandoori prawns

SERVES 3–4

15–20 large prawns (shrimp), peeled and
    deveined
2 tbsp tomato paste
½ tsp red chilli powder
1 tbsp cooking oil, plus extra
    for cooking
1 tsp garlic powder
½ tsp tamarind powder or
    amchur powder
large pinch of turmeric powder
1 tbsp fresh lemon juice
salt and freshly ground black pepper
lemon wedges, to serve
freshly chopped coriander, to serve

Prawns can handle strong flavours and are never happier than when partnered with red chilli and garlic.

In a large bowl, combine all the ingredients, except the prawns (shrimp) and lemon juice. Add the prawns (shrimp) and stir gently to coat. Set aside to marinate for 15–20 minutes.

Place the prawns (shrimp) on a heated, lightly oiled griddle and cook on the hob for 2–3 minutes on each side, until they turn crisp and are cooked through.

Drizzle with fresh lemon juice and serve with lemon wedges and a sprinkle of fresh coriander.

Paneer and potato curry

SERVES 3–4

2 tbsp vegetable oil
1 tsp minced ginger
1 large onion, finely chopped
1 large tomato, finely chopped
1 tbsp tomato paste
1–2 green chillies, seeds included,
    finely chopped
½ tsp red chilli powder
large pinch of turmeric powder
1 tsp coriander powder
2 medium potatoes, peeled and cut
    into bite-sized pieces
240 ml (1 cup) water
450 g (1 lb) paneer, cut into
    bite-sized cubes
salt, to season

This vegetarian curry uses paneer – a firm, white, unsalted cheese that is easy to make at home by straining boiled milk and a little lemon juice through a fine sieve or cheese cloth.

Heat the oil in a large pan and sauté the ginger and onion until softened and lightly browned. Add the tomato, tomato paste, chillies and spices, and cook until the tomato starts to break down and blend with the other ingredients.

Add the potatoes and water, season with salt, and cook, covered, for 10–15 minutes until the potatoes are tender.

Stir in the paneer and cook for another 5–6 minutes, until the potatoes are completely cooked through.

Serve as part of a main meal, or with naan bread and steamed basmati rice.

SOHO

Soho is one of the best-known and most visited areas of London, with a long, illustrious and colourful history. Despite its central location, Soho has always been more bohemian than its high-class neighbouring locales of Mayfair, Marylebone and St James, attracting courtesans, artisans and immigrants drawn from across the continent over the centuries. However, it is French, Italian and Greek settlers that have probably had the greatest impact on the area over the years and have helped to shape its unique character, especially during the 1700s and 1800s.

This has resulted in a truly cosmopolitan square mile that is home to hundreds of cafes, bars, restaurants and shops that span a global remit. And while Soho is a hub of creativity and diversity, with media studios, achingly cool bars and its proud claim to be the heartland of London's LGBT scene, much of it is still steeped in history and the traditional happily coexists with modern influences. Berwick Street is a great example of this: the street itself is a happy hybrid of concept bars, trendy shops and more traditional pubs, while the market caters to the daily grocery shopper and the street food enthusiast in one long row of stalls. Open all day Monday to Saturday, you can fill up your basket with fruit and veg, or grab a falafel or deli steak sandwich.

The Italian influence is obvious as you travel around Soho with cafes such as Bar Italia acting as a focal point for the community. This family-run coffee bar and restaurant has been servicing Soho's caffeine craving since 1949 – for 22 hours a day (the café shuts briefly between 5am and 7am before it opens again for breakfast). There are also a number of excellent Italian delis, with Camisa & Sons and Lina Stores being particularly worthy of mention. They have been doing business in Soho since 1961 and 1940 respectively and offer the full range of Italian speciality foods, as well as prepared dishes, antipasti and fresh coffee.

Meanwhile, if you want to sample French baking, Maison Bertaux offers a lesson in both history and patisserie. Having resided in its Greek Street location since 1871, the café can claim to have witnessed firsthand the gentrification of Soho and watched it change dramatically through the ages. For a more formal introduction to the delights of French cuisine, try L'Escargot – the oldest French bistro in London – or the below-ground homage to Paris, Brasserie Zédel, with its opulent interior but incredibly wallet-friendly fare.

Tottenham Court Road

Tube

3, 12, 14, 19, 38, 94

Bus

Coq au vin

50 g (½ cup) plain (all-purpose) flour

1½ tsp salt

pinch of freshly ground black pepper

1 x 1.4–1.6 kg (3–3½ lb) whole chicken,
    cut into 8 pieces

6 thick slices of bacon

6 whole pearl onions, peeled

2 garlic cloves, finely chopped

100 g (1 cup) roughly chopped celery

225 g (1½ cups) roughly chopped carrot

225 g (1½ cups) sliced mushrooms

225 ml (1 cup) chicken stock

225 ml (1 cup) dry white wine

½ tsp dried thyme

1 bay leaf

2 tbsp finely chopped parsley

Soho has a long-standing love affair with France; a fact reaffirmed by the profusion of French restaurants and patisseries in this vibrant square mile in central London. This classic dish pays homage to the area's Gallic history.

In a small bowl, combine the flour with 1 teaspoon of the salt, and the pepper. Clean the chicken and pat dry with paper towel. Coat the chicken pieces evenly with the seasoned flour and set aside.

In a large Dutch oven or heavy-based saucepan with lid, fry the bacon over a medium-high heat until crisp. Transfer to a plate covered with a paper towel to drain.

Brown the chicken on all sides in the bacon fat. Add the onions, garlic, celery, carrot and mushrooms, stirring for about 8–10 minutes, until the onions are tender. Drain the fat from the Dutch oven.

Crumble the bacon and add to the chicken and vegetables. Add the chicken stock, wine, the remaining salt, thyme, bay leaf and parsley to the Dutch oven. Reduce the heat to low, cover and simmer for 1 hour, or until the chicken is tender.

Remove the bay leaf before serving.

Punch Room
EDITION punch

SERVES 1

50 ml (3 tbsp) Plymouth gin
2.5 ml (½ tsp) Benedictine Dom
25 ml (1½ tbsp) maple syrup
drop of orange flower water
25 ml (1½ tbsp) lemon juice
75 ml (⅓ cup) jasmine tea
jasmine flowers, to garnish
lemon slice, to garnish

Punch Room is a reservation-only bar tucked away inside The London EDITION hotel on the north border of Soho. The opulent interior is perfectly suited to enjoying a leisurely cocktail or two, away from the frenetic London thoroughfares outside. The oak-panelled room takes its inspiration from manor house libraries and opulent private clubs. EDITION Punch is the bar's signature drink; this recipe is designed as a single serving but you can multiply the ingredients to make a bowlful of punch for a party.

'Punch is the ultimate drink for a summer party. If created well it is tasty, refreshing and also designed for sharing. Punch requires little maintenance and will allow the host of the party to enjoy the evening rather than making drinks all night and also not pressuring guests to make their own drinks so everyone can enjoy the evening.'

Davide Segat, Bar Manager

Build the ingredients into a punch glass over plenty of ice.

Garnish with jasmine flowers and a lemon slice.

MEET THE PRODUCERS

London is a city bursting at the seams with creativity, innovation and entrepreneurial spirit And this is particularly apparent when it comes to the artisan food scene.

From craft brewers and distillers to cheesemakers, meat smokers, chocolatiers and bakers, an increasing number of food producers are choosing to base their businesses in the capital and London is all the richer for their presence.

With a captive local clientele keen to buy top-quality produce with just a handful of food miles, there is a sense of pride and a great deal of support from Londoners but also among the producers themselves. Many work in close proximity to each other, in order to share their skills, experience and infrastructure. In the process, they have created production enclaves across the capital – hubs of culinary creativity that are thriving and growing as more people turn sidelines and passions into full-time jobs.

The Kernel Brewery

01 Spa Business Park, Spa Road SE16 4QT

+44 (0)20 7231 4516 / www.thekernelbrewery.com

There has been a huge resurgence in craft beer production in the capital in recent years. Although we're still some way off from returning to the halcyon days of hundreds of independent breweries scattered around the capital, much progress has been made and there are now over 70 breweries in London, as drinkers become more discerning and discover the huge variety of lagers, ales, bitters and stouts that are being produced on a small to medium scale – each with their own unique production techniques and characteristics.

When Evin O'Riordain made the leap from home brewer to professional brewer, the London craft beer industry was still very much in its infancy. The interest in brewing came about when he was helping to set up a cheese shop in New York and, although fromagerie to brewery might seem worlds apart, he points out the many similarities in expertise required for both trades, such as an instinctive knowledge of when the product is ready and acute senses of smell and taste.

Despite a love of beer, it was cheese that initially drew the Irishman to London in 1999, when he joined Neal's Yard Dairy. Here, he honed his cheesemonger's skills while experimenting with brewing beer at home. When his kitchen could no longer handle the quantities, Evin found premises on Druid Street and The Kernel Brewery was born.

The move down the road to Spa Terminus came about in 2012 when the company needed to upsize its operation. It also coincided with a desire to distance the business from the increasingly busy Ropewalk food market, where retail business had taken precedence over distribution. A number of other wholesale-based businesses also made the move to Spa Terminus at the same time and this likeminded collective continues to support each other, often cross-selling products to the restaurant and catering industries.

The 13-strong team at The Kernel brews its range of eight or so beers five days a week and sells kegs directly to bars and restaurants, with bottles available for retail sale direct from the brewery on a Saturday morning. Demand is such that Evin could upscale the operation and take the brewery to the next level of production. However, that would mean moving again and changing the dynamic of the business, which isn't something he's keen to explore.

'We're happy here, we've got a great team and we love what we do. Why change that?'

Pale ale vegetable tempura

SERVES 4 AS A SNACK

2 red bell peppers, cut into slices or rings
8 baby corn, sliced in half lengthways
1 large carrot, cut into large batons
½ head broccoli, broken into florets
sunflower oil, for deep-frying
soy or chilli sauce, to serve

FOR THE BATTER:
75 g (¾ cup) plain (all-purpose) flour
pinch of salt
200 ml (¾ cup) Kernel Pale Ale

Pale ale is the perfect ingredient for light, crispy tempura. Use it straight from the fridge, as the batter needs to be cold.

Prepare the batter. Sieve the flour and salt into a large bowl. Take the pale ale from the fridge and beat into the flour, until the batter is smooth – don't over whisk.

Heat the oil in a large pan. It needs to reach 190°C (375°F).

In batches, dip the vegetables into the batter, shake off any excess then carefully place into the oil. Fry for 2–3 minutes until the batter is golden, then remove with a slotted spoon. Place the cooked vegetables on kitchen paper to drain.

Repeat with the remaining vegetables and serve with soy or chilli sauce.

Wildes Cheese

+44 (0)7758 755 248

www.wildescheese.co.uk

In 2011 the dark clouds of recession reached the north London borough of Tottenham. The knock-on effect led to Philip Wilton being made redundant and it was this life-changing event that sparked the move to become an urban cheesemaker. Philip had always harboured a dream to make cheese but couldn't imagine how it could work without leaving the city and moving to a country idyll.

Plans for the business were formulated during a trip to Las Vegas – an unlikely spot to spark a cheese revolution – but timing wasn't perfect for Philip and his partner Keith Sides. They returned to Tottenham in the aftermath of the London riots, with people trying to persuade them that inner city London wasn't ready for artisan cheese and they should rethink their plans. However, as they watched the local community get their brooms out and begin a collective clean-up, they became convinced that they should stay put and set up the business in their back yard. This was pretty much literally, as the pair took out a lease on a tiny unit in a local industrial estate in 2012 and founded Wildes Cheese. Philip's first instinct proved correct – in a city that loves to eat, there's always room for new producers creating quality products.

Wildes produces a stock range of about ten cheeses, including Wilderella – an American-style mozzarella; fresh curd cheese; The Londonshire – a medium, soft cheese; and Barnsbury – a traditional English cheese that matures for at least two months.

As the proud recipient of a number of awards – including Winner of London's Favourite Cheese, and Slow Food London Cheesemaker of the Year 2015 (runner up) – Philip has achieved a great deal in the short time since the business was founded. He loves meeting customers and regularly mans the Wildes' cheese stall that has a pitch at various London food markets – Tottenham Green Market, Alexandra Palace Farmers' Market and Enfield Market to name a few. The cheese is also for sale in the online shop and in a number of delis and cafes in North London.

'I made the decision that I was going to change my life; become someone else; do something useful. I had always wanted to make something I could point to and be proud of.'

Wildes
Urban grilled cheese rarebit

SERVES 1

50 ml (¼ cup) London dark beer

1 tsp English mustard

2 tbsp butter, plus extra for bread

2 tsp Worcestershire sauce

150 g (5 oz) St Bruce and Howard
    Cheese, grated

2 medium free-range egg yolks

4 thick slices fresh sourdough bread

2 tsp bacon jam (use onion jam for a veggie
    sandwich) or chutney

salt and freshly ground black pepper, to
    season

If you prefer a saltier flavour and crumblier texture, use St Bruce and Highcross cheese. For the beer, I recommend either Redemption Brewery Fellowship Porter or Beavertown Black Betty.

Add the beer and mustard into a small pan and mix to a paste. Add the butter and Worcestershire sauce and heat gently until the butter has melted.

Add the grated cheese and stir to melt but don't allow it to boil.

Once the paste is smooth, season with salt and pepper, remove from the heat and allow to cool until just warm.

Beat in the egg yolks and check the seasoning.

Butter the bread slices on one side and lay buttered-side down on a chopping board. Spread the bacon jam thickly over the bread and add the cheese paste to 2 of the slices.

Place the remaining bread, buttered-side up, on top of the cheese.

Heat a heavy-based frying pan to medium. Place the sandwiches in the pan and cook for 3–4 minutes until golden and crispy, pressing down occasionally with a spatula. Turn the sandwiches over and repeat. Serve immediately.

Bermondsey Street Bees

+44 (0)7876 790689

www.bermondseystreetbees.co.uk

When it comes to changing career, you'd be hard-pressed to find a bigger transition than that of Bermondsey Bees' founder Dale Gibson. In 2007, Dale switched from stockbroker to beekeeper, setting up his beehives on the roof of the Victorian sugar mill on Bermondsey Street that became the family home following a move south of the river two years previously.

Although the move from finance to farming was a huge shift, Dale also believes there's an element of overlap between the two careers. 'My City background does inform my very organised approach to the business of beekeeping, so in some ways the two jobs are not as different as you might imagine!'

In terms of location, Dale couldn't have picked a better spot. With Borough Market just down the road and Maltby Street beginning to carve out a culinary niche in the area when they arrived, Bermondsey Bees fitted neatly into the local burgeoning artisan food scene. As for the bees, they settled in to their surroundings, foraging from Bermondsey roof terraces, as well as the many parks, allotments and gardens scattered around the area. The native and exotic pollen and nectar they gather on their travels gives the honey its unique and award-winning flavour.

The business is a family venture, with Dale's wife Sarah running all the marketing and retail and Sarah is kept increasingly busy as more restaurants and retailers appreciate the quality of this completely raw and unprocessed honey. As well as supplying a lot of honey to beer brewer, Hiver Beer (another local producer), Bermondsey Street Honey is also stocked in delis such as Soho Farmhouse, Honey & Co and Sourced Market, as well as Selfridges Food Hall. It is also available to buy at the company's weekly Maltby Street stall.

Having been voted Small Artisan Producer of the Year at the 2016 Great Taste Awards, this successful London food enterprise is captivating the taste buds of everyone who samples its urban honey.

'People are amazed that you can live in central London, right in the shadow of The Shard, and still be an actual farmer, producing real food of the highest quality.'

BERMONDSEY STREET BEES

UNION RAW HONEY · METRO RAW HONEY · FRENCH RAW HONEY

Bermondsey Street Bees

Chilled tomato soup

SERVES 6

1 large cucumber (skin on), chopped into
    5-mm (¼-in) cubes

1 spring onion (scallion), finely chopped

1–2 garlic cloves, roughly crushed and
    chopped

2 tsp clear raw honey

½ tsp dried dill

1 ltr (4 cups) fresh tomato juice (or good-
    quality readymade tomato juice)

250 ml (1 cup) natural yogurt (and/or sour
    cream, to taste)

1 red bell pepper, finely chopped

6–10 button mushrooms, thinly sliced

salt and freshly ground black pepper, to
    season

watercress sprigs, to garnish

fresh dill, to garnish

Although surprising at first glance, this is an amazingly easy and delicious summer soup in which honey plays an essential role, uniting the savoury ingredients and giving the soup a silky texture. Full flavoured and built around a classic combination of honey and dill, this recipe originates from Australia in the 1950s. It has been passed down through three generations, each tweaking it to achieve their perfect taste and texture. Feel free to do the same – none of the quantities need be exact. Combine all the ingredients in a large bowl and mix well. Season to taste with salt and pepper.

Cover and chill in the fridge for several hours.

Divide between serving bowls and garnish with watercress sprigs and fresh dill.

Crown & Queue Meats

Arch 8, Spa Business Park, Dockley Road SE16 3FJ

www.curedmeats.london

Founder and Managing Director of Crown & Queue Meats, Adrienne Eiser Treeby worked as a professional chef for 16 years before undertaking a three-year salumi apprenticeship where she learned to butcher and cure meat. This was followed by another three years working in cheese affinage (ageing and maturing cheese). So, by 2014, Adrienne had all the experience required to start her own meat-curing company.

Adrienne believes food production is a community effort and she works closely with farmers and suppliers to produce dry-cured sausages made only from High-Welfare British Heritage pork and indigenous English herbs, as well as other locally produced ingredients.

Adrienne chose this corner of London to set up her business, as it's a hub of culinary creativity. 'South-east London is where it's at! Not just in terms of food production but also in terms of atmosphere. I work next to some of the best foodies London has to offer. I also love the community – it can be hard work to produce food in an urban environment, so we food producers care for and carry each other in a way unlike anywhere else.'

Having worked all over the world, Adrienne believes that food takes on a certain flavour (what the French call *terroir*) from where it's made and Bermondsey has a unique flavour. Producing food in the capital also cuts down on the carbon footprint: it means that Crown & Queue can offer its customers top-quality products that are produced on their doorstep.

As more producers set up shop in the capital and supply restaurants and retail customers with locally produced food, so London gains kudos. 'It's sad that England has suffered a bad culinary reputation,' says Adrienne. 'It makes me proud to be a respected food producer in the city, and know that I'm helping change people's minds about the glory of British foods.'

Although primarily a wholesale business, you can buy Crown & Queue cured sausages from their production space most Saturdays, or order from their online shop. They're also busy on London's market scene, making regular appearances at Oval, Woolwich Royal Arsenal, Alexandra Palace and Wendell Park.

'I love being so close to all my customers. I think it is immensely satisfying to my retail customers that they can come and visit me anytime and really, truly, know where their food comes from.'

Crown & Queue Meats
Cobnut parcels

SERVES 4

4 damsons (or greengages or
    Victoria plums), halved and stones
    removed
½ tsp finely chopped fresh root ginger
1 sprig fresh rosemary, picked and
    finely chopped
1 garlic clove, finely chopped
100 g (3½ oz) cobnuts (in the husk),
    shelled and coarsely chopped
squeeze of lemon juice
1 tbsp warm butter (or as necessary)
75 g (3 oz) Crown & Queue's Black-pepper
    Cured Pork Belly, thinly sliced
salt and freshly ground black pepper, to
    season

Cobnuts are a variety of hazelnut that are usually in season from August to September when you can buy them fresh, still in their husks.
Preheat the oven to 180°C (350°F).

Slice a little circle off the bottom of the damsons so they sit flat, with their stone holes on top.

In a small bowl, combine the ginger, rosemary, garlic and cobnuts. Add the lemon juice, butter and season with salt and pepper to taste. The butter should cover the mixture well without being too greasy. Add a little more, if necessary.

Spoon the mixture into the damsons so they are mounded slightly. Carefully lay slices of cured pork belly over each damson half.

Place the parcels on a parchment-covered baking sheet and bake until the belly begins to soften and melt and the stuffing is hot (about 8–10 minutes).

Increase the heat to 220°C (425°F) (and switch to grill setting, if possible). Continue to cook until the belly begins to crisp and the plums begin to sizzle. Serve warm.

The Slow Bread Company

Arch 65, Stamford Brook Arches W6 0TQ

+44 (0)20 8748 8486 / www.slowbreadcompany.co.uk

Nick May has been baking bread for friends and family for many years. However, when his wife took a couple of loaves into work one day, little did she realise that it would change the course of both their lives. The bread was so well received that Nick abandoned a 25-year publishing career to bake full time. The Slow Bread Company was officially founded in 2013 and the couple haven't looked back.

They produce traditional sourdough – or naturally leavened – loaves that use an ancient Dorset starter and locally produced, unbleached flour. The dough has a long fermentation period of up to 24 hours and everything is baked fresh to order. The micro bakery also makes scones, focaccia, baguettes and bagels – all free from preservatives and added fats, just the way it should be.

Nick chose west London when he found the perfect premises in an area with the right demographics. 'However fashionable east London is these days, there is still plenty of demand in west London.' However, the bread isn't just enjoyed in Chiswick – delis, pubs and restaurants around the capital have caught on to the high-quality, handmade loaves and buns that are baked with love in Nick's bakery.

'The capital has been an open and outward-looking city for the last two thousand years, with an incredible depth of talent and influences.'

The Slow Bread Company
Cobb club sandwich

SERVES 1

2 spring onions (scallions), finely chopped

50 g (2 oz) Gorgonzola

1 tbsp fresh mayonnaise

2 slices streaky bacon or prosciutto

2 slices fresh sourdough, ciabatta or
   baguette

50 g (2 oz) cooked chicken, sliced

½ avocado, sliced

1 vine tomato, sliced

At The Slow Bread Company, we believe this is by far the best sandwich in the world. You can adjust the amounts of ingredients to suit your taste. Before you tackle this mammoth lunchtime treat, pour a large glass of wine, switch off your phone and lock the door – this needs your full attention.

Mix the spring onions (scallions), Gorgonzola and mayonnaise together in a small bowl. Chill in the fridge.

Dry fry the bacon or prosciutto in a small frying pan, until crispy.

Lay out the bread, place some sliced chicken, avocado and tomato on one slice. Place the bacon on top and finish with the Gorgonzola mixture.

Carefully lay the other piece of bread on top, slice in half, if liked, and enjoy.

England Preserves

www.englandpreserves.co.uk

Sky Cracknell and Kai Knutsen founded England Preserves in 2001 and the company is another success story in the foodie enclave of Spa Terminus; a cluster of likeminded, independent food producers a stone's throw from Borough Market.

While Kai always had half an eye on the food industry as a long-term career – he worked in the industry on leaving school before becoming an art student and working in media – Sky was heading towards a career in design when they met. That was in 1999 in Borough Market (then just a small monthly market) where they were inspired by the renewed appreciation of an English food culture and indigenous ingredients.

The pair feels privileged to have carved out their company's niche in this foodie corner of the capital. 'It's amazing to have the opportunity to be part of a food community like Spa Terminus; not only for inspiration but also the pooling of knowledge,' says Sky.

Due to their hard work, experimentation with ingredients and endless pursuit of excellence, England Preserves are now sought out and sold in delis and farm shops across the UK, as well as being the pickles, chutneys, jams and marmalades of choice for an increasing number of cafes, hotels and restaurants.

Seasonality is vitally important to Sky and Kai, as are provenance and preparation – the preserves are all cooked by hand and include locally sourced fruit and vegetables, and the jams all have a low sugar and high fruit content. For toast and scones, there's Raspberry Deluxe, aromatic Cherry Amour and delicate Bermondsey Bramble. While sandwiches, ploughmans and quiches pair wonderfully with chutneys such as Pear, Date & Ale (the ale in this chutney comes from neighbour The Kernel Brewery, see page 190), Red Onion Marmalade or the piquant Piccalilli.

'I love the diversity of London, as the calibre of food producers is so high and there is inspiration around every corner. I never forget how fortunate we are to be part of it or just how unique it is.'

'We like to eat these scones (page 212) warm. Serve with England Preserves jam and clotted cream, which seems to be available in every small shop these days. They also freeze very well so don't be put off making them if you are home alone – take them out one at a time whenever you fancy one.'

England Preserves
Homemade scones

1 egg

pinch of salt

450 g (3 ²/₃ cups) self-raising flour

handful of wholemeal (whole-wheat) flour

100 g (½ cup) unsalted butter from the fridge, cut into cubes

100 g (½ cup) granulated sugar

150 g (1 cup) sultanas (golden raisins)

300 ml (1¼ cups) buttermilk

The homemade scone is as different to its commercial relative as chalk is to cheese. Best of all, you can be eating one, warm from the oven, less than an hour after you've pulled the mixing bowl from the cupboard.

You can apply a multitude of tweaks to this recipe to suit your personal preference. I always make mine with a handful of wholemeal flour, buttermilk and some plump sultanas. The flour could just as easily be rye or buckwheat; and you can use whole milk instead of buttermilk, or a combination of milk and natural yogurt. Add in the fruit or leave it out, or flavour with lemon zest or cinnamon – the options are infinite.

Preheat the oven to 220°C (425°F).

Break the egg into a bowl with a tiny pinch of salt and mix together. Cover a couple of baking sheets with non-stick baking paper or butter them.

In a large bowl, rub the flours and butter together with your fingertips until you have a fine crumb. Mix through the sugar and sultanas (golden raisins).

Make a well in the centre of the mixture and pour in the buttermilk. If you have one, use a palette knife to bring the mixture together. Don't knead the dough; it should be very soft without being sticky. If sticky, add a small amount of flour; if crumbly, add milk 1 teaspoon at a time.

Flour the work surface and tip out the dough. Press down on the dough to flatten to about 3 cm (1 in). Using a 5-cm (2-in) cutter, cut the scones and place on the baking sheets.

Brush the tops with the egg glaze. Place the scones in the oven and bake for 12–15 minutes. When cooked, the scones will be golden brown on top. Transfer to a cooling rack to cool

Jensen's Gin

Bermondsey Distillery, 55 Stanworth Street SE1 3NY

www.bermondseygin.com

Founder Christian Jensen moved to London from Denmark and turned his borderline obsession with vintage gin (he has over 900 bottles in his collection) into a hobby when he began creating old-fashioned styles of gin at home. In 2004, the hobby became a business and Bermondsey Gin was born. Fast-forward to 2013: distiller Dr Anne Brock and International Brand Ambassador Hannah Lanfear joined the company, the business moved to Stanworth Street and the team began to distil independently.

With a background in organic chemistry and a PhD from Oxford University, Anne chose the heady world of distilling over a more staid career in pharmaceuticals and swiftly took over the management of the distillery – once she had project managed the build. Meanwhile, Hannah left behind years of managing bars and training bartenders to bring her encyclopaedic knowledge of classic cocktails and historic gin to the business.

When the company first started out, there were very few old-fashioned gins on the market – Christian wanted to recreate the true character of the older style, which is subtler and more complex. The location of the distillery was important and he chose Bermondsey partly because of its rich history and long association with the gin trade. Gin distilleries dotted the area in the 1700s and the spirit has played an important role in the history of London – from the devastating gin epidemic to the fortunes of foreign trade. However, gin suffered a demise and the distilleries gradually disappeared over the centuries, so it seemed fitting to reinvigorate the sector by setting up a new, independent distillery in the area.

Jensen's has proved popular with gin connoisseurs and is now available in many cocktail bars, pubs and restaurants around London. As word spreads, Jensen's is becoming more widely available across the UK and further afield. The brand is particularly popular with bartenders looking to create classic cocktails with an authentic flavour. You can also enjoy Jensen's Gin at the distillery when it opens to the public as part of the Maltby Street weekend market.

Old Tom Negroni

SERVES 1

25 ml (2 tbsp) Jensen's Old Tom
25 ml (2 tbsp) Martini Rosso
25 ml (2 tbsp) Campari
orange slice, to garnish

Negroni cocktails are traditionally served as aperitifs.

Build the drink in a rocks glass.

Garnish with a thick orange slice.

Ramos gin fizz

SERVES 1

50 ml (3 tbsp) Jensen's Old Tom
10 ml (2 tsp) fresh lemon juice
10 ml (2 tsp) fresh lime juice
30 ml (2 tbsp) simple syrup
25 ml (2 tbsp) double (heavy) cream
25 ml (2 tbsp) egg white
5 ml (1 tsp) Luxardo maraschino liqueur
dash of orange blossom water

Jensen's Old Tom is made to a recipe from the 1840s.

Pour all the ingredients into a cocktail shaker and shake very hard for 3 minutes.

Strain into a highball and top with soda.

Simple syrup
To make a simple syrup, add equal amounts of sugar and water to a small pan and heat until the sugar has fully dissolved. Allow to cool then use the required amount in the cocktail.

The Green Park

SERVES 1

50 ml (3 tbsp) Jensen's Old Tom
25 ml (2 tbsp) fresh lemon juice
12.5 ml (1 tbsp) simple syrup
3 drops celery bitters
25 ml (2 tbsp) egg white
5 basil leaves

This cocktail was created by Erik Lorincz of The Savoy.

Pour all the ingredients into a cocktail shaker and shake hard.

Strain into a coupette.

London Food Events

JANUARY
Chinese New Year

FEBRUARY
London Gin Festival

MARCH
London Drinker Beer & Cider Festival
IFE Exhibition

APRIL
World Street Food Festival
London Coffee Festival
Bavarian Beerhouse Spring Festival

MAY
Foodies Festival Syon Park
The Spring Haze Beer Festival
Artisan Wine Fair

JUNE
Taste of London
Gefiltefest London Jewish Food Festival
Ealing Midsummer Fayre
Gelato Festival

JULY
Foodies Festival Blackheath
Carnaby Street Eat
Eid Festival
Soho Food Feast
Lambeth Country Show
Feast @ Fitzrovia
Urban Food Fest
Waterloo Quarter Food Festival
Sephardi Festival

AUGUST
London Craft Beer Festival
BBC Good Food Festival
London Halal Food Festival
Chinese Food Festival
The Great British Beer Festival
Gin Festival
Foodies Festival Alexandra Palace

SEPTEMBER
Meatopia London
Eat the World
Grillstock
Tooting Foodival
London Chill Festival

OCTOBER
Chocolate Week
Oktoberfest
London Restaurant Festival
UK RumFest
BBC Good Food Cake & Bake Show
VegFest UK
Urban Food Fest

NOVEMBER
BBC Good Food Show
Taste of London Winter

DECEMBER
Chocolate Festival
The Christmas StockingMKT

Index

Index of recipes

Picture Credits

Jemma Watts (pages 4, 6, 15, 22, 27, 29, 31, 34, 55, 56, 57, 67, 70, 74, 83, 87, 93, 94, 97, 99, 102, 105, 106, 111, 114, 117, 121, 124, 132, 137, 141, 159, 162, 167, 170, 200, 219)

David Munns (pages 16, 21, 24, 32, 37, 40, 61, 64, 68, 73, 76, 80, 100, 108, 113, 122, 127, 131, 139, 142, 145, 149, 157, 160, 165, 172, 177, 180, 184, 187, 190, 195, 199, 203, 206, 211)

Gavin Robinson (pages 67, 74, 111, 141, 155, 162, 167, 175, 178, 183)

Ian Garlic (pages 134, 168)

Tony Briscoe (page 168)

Alamy (page 15): Vladislav Gajic; (page 18): Francisco A. Soeiro; (page 22): Hemis ; (page 128): Stephen Chung; (page 128): John Norman; (page 128): Coaster; (page 183): Nick Moore; (page 183): Mark Beton/Capital; (page 224): Brian England.

Getty Images (page 34): LatitudeStock - Flo Smith; (page 155): Ands 456; (page 155): Madzia71

Istock (page 128): Alphotographic; (page 128): Chris Dorney; (page 183): DavidCallan

Shutterstock (page155): Elena Rostunova

Additional photography

The Ivy (page 18): exterior David Griffen; interior Jake Eastham

Fortnum & Mason (page 38): Grant Smith, Phil Harris

Le Gavroche (page 43): Issy Croker

Barrafina (page 74): John Carey

Lyle's (page 103): Interior Anton Rodriguez; food Per-Anders Jorgensen

The Marksman (page 111): dining room Jorge Monedero; front view Ali Mobasser; terrace Miria Harris; waiter station Anabel Navarro

London Farmers' Markets (page 146): Cheryl Cohen; Farah Syed; Lissy Prinzi; Claudia Marinaro

Street Feast (page 9, 149): Scott Grummett; Johnny Stephens, Chris Coulson

Kernel Brewery (page 191): Michael Kelly

Bermondsey Bees (page 199): Bermondsey Bees

Wildes Cheese (page 195): Chris Terry

Jensen's Gin (page 213, 214): Addie Chinn

Portland (page 62): Keiko Oikawa